Books in Print by Marie Chapian

Teens:

Am I the Only One Here With Faded Genes?
Feeling Small/Walking Tall

Biography:

Back on Course (Gavin McLeod Story)
Forgive Me (Cathy Crowell Webb story)
Help Me Remember, Help Me Forget
Of Whom the World Was Not Worthy

Christian Living:

Close Friendships: Making Them, Keeping Them
Free To Be Thin
Love and Be Loved
Mothers and Daughters
Slimming Down and Growing Up
Staying Happy in an Unhappy World
Telling Yourself the Truth
There's More to Being Thin Than Being Thin
Why Do I Do What I Don't Want to Do?

Devotional:

Discovering Joy
His Gifts to Me
His Thoughts Toward Me
Making His Heart Glad
Discovering Joy
The Secret Place of Strength

Video:

Fun to Be Fit

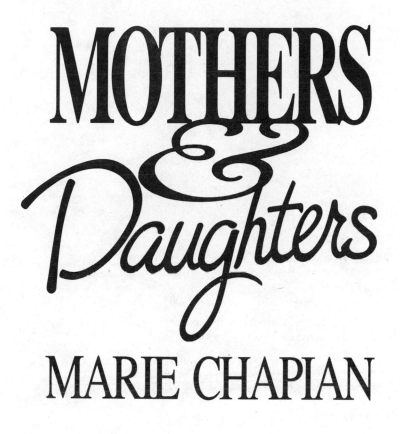

MOTHERS & Daughters

MARIE CHAPIAN

BETHANY HOUSE PUBLISHERS
MINNEAPOLIS, MINNESOTA 55438
A Division of Bethany Fellowship, Inc.

Published by Bethany House Publishers
A Division of Bethany Fellowship, Inc.
6820 Auto Club Road, Minneapolis, Minnesota 55438

Printed in the United States of America

Library of Congress Cataloging-in-Publication Data

Chapian, Marie.
    Mothers and daughters / Marie Chapian.
        p.   cm.

    1. Mothers and daughters—United States—Case studies.
2. Parenting—United States—Case studies.
3. Teenage girls—United States—Family relationships—Case studies.
I. Title.
HQ755.85.C485   1988
306.8'743—dc19   88-4199
ISBN 1-55661-007-6 (pbk.)   CIP

To Christa and Liza
Because you came to me, my babies,
I've seen the smile of God.
Because you came to me, my little girls,
I've seen the hand of God.
Because you came to me, my daughters,
I've seen the arm of God.
Because you are my friends today,
I know the heart of God.

Marie, Christa and Liza Chapian

MARIE CHAPIAN, Ph.D. , known and loved around the world as an inspirational author and speaker, has written over twenty-five books with translations in thirteen languages. She has received many awards for her writing, including the Evangelical Christian Publishing Association Gold Medallion Award and the *Cornerstone* Book of the Year Award.

PREFACE

by Liza Chapian

When I was about eight years old I got the chicken pox. I was really sick. I had itchy bumps and blisters every-where—between my toes, behind my ears, in my mouth. When they finally went away, I broke out with a brand new case of them, only worse. I remember my mom painting white medicine all over me and sitting by my side. She told me funny stories, complete with costumes and funny faces, to cheer me up. She invented activities like banquets and parties for my stuffed animals and me, and I can still see her sweeping into the room with plates and bowls and soup and treats and party favors. There I sat, miserably covered in red spots, surrounded by teddy bears in party hats having juice and soup while my mother, dressed as Chief Feather-duster, danced around the room singing me outrageous songs about birds getting stuck in her headdress.

When medicine didn't work, she figured laughter would. And she was right.

Whenever I cried *Mommy*, she was there. Whenever I was sick, she gave me lots of attention and love. But that wasn't unusual, for she gave me attention and love all the time. I didn't have to get sick to receive special treatment.

Her stories and costumes and songs were a regular part of our life. She took my sister and me most places with her and it seemed like no matter where we went, it was fun and an adventure for us. Going to the store and the laundromat were like special events, celebrations even. And best were our excursions to art museums, to the library, and the incredible picnics in the middle of the city.

So when I think of growing up as a daughter, I have good and happy memories. But when I was ending my junior high years, things began to change. Suddenly Mommy was no longer the center of my universe. I discovered a whole new world of independent thinking and choice making.

And not only did I begin to think more and more about what I wanted, I thought about what I didn't want. I wanted to be my own person; I didn't want to be restricted. I wanted to make my own decisions; I didn't want to be told what to do. My mother's rules that once were OK were now a huge offense. Now I felt that obeying her rules without question, or at least an argument, was like losing myself, my rights, my identity.

It seemed to me that my mother was always getting in my way. I figured she just didn't want me to have any fun. She was definitely not "in."

I read every Christian teenage book on how to grow up successfully. But no book explained what was happening to me. I really wanted to be older. My thoughts and desires were all centered in things I wasn't old enough to do. How was I supposed to grow up? How was I supposed to be my *own* person? If I became an obedient little daughter and did everything my mom told me to do, I just knew I'd be giving up my right to be *me*.

Here I was, a Christian girl, raised in a Christian home, always in church and Sunday school; I went to Christian camps, Christian Bible clubs—Christian everything. My mother and Christa and I were a close family, and Mom really lived and showed us how loving and faithful the Lord

Jesus is. I genuinely loved the Lord, but now I was discovering an exciting, forbidden world where there was *dancing*, movies, parties, fashion magazines of beautiful girls with perfect skin photographed with gorgeous guys; there was the beach, boys, things my mother said were sin. How could I possibly comprehend that this new glamorous, happy world was sin?

The only answer I could come up with was that my mother was the one who was messed up. She was too strict, too uptight. She was just out of it.

I was still going to church, of course, but it was no longer fun. It was a huge effort and I complained and argued and tried to get out of it. In youth group there would be adults who came to give testimonies; so here comes a beautiful lady all dressed up, her hair perfect and all, and she tells us with tears in her eyes, "I did it *all*, young people. I got into drinking, drugs, you name it. I had great times, but now I realize it all meant nothing. I had everything the world can offer, but still I was unsatisfied. Money, sex, fame and fun parties didn't give me what I really wanted. Oh sure, it was terrific for a while, but now I have found Jesus."

I would sit there and think that I'd like to try a little of that fun she was talking about. Obviously, Jesus was for old people or burned-out adults after they've had all the fun.

Me, I was only fourteen, far too young for Jesus.

Looking at my mom's life didn't give me much incentive either. As long as I could remember, she worked day and night for what I could see had no rewards at all. For years I had gone to sleep to the sound of her typewriter, and in the morning she was still typing away. My mom's life seemed unglamorous with church, meetings, teaching, supporting a family—nothing like the new carefree and exciting life I wanted.

So there I was, a daughter, living in my parent's home, going to school, trying to live to the fullest, but I had this continual interference going. It was my mother's love. I acted horribly and she continued to love me! Every doubt I had about God, she contradicted with a word of wisdom or with her kindness. It made me angry. I was happier if she'd be unpleasant. But she waited up for me when I came stumbling in the door in the late hours of the night. She was there for me. There were no teddy bears and hats, but she was there.

It made me mad when she prayed for me, because I was afraid God was on her side, and in order to be right with Him, I figured I'd have to give up my friends and having fun. But strangely enough, it wasn't as much fun as I thought it promised. When the people I thought were my friends betrayed me, who was there for me? My mom. I became disillusioned by the fantasy the world offered me. The lie I had believed almost did me in—but not quite.

I can talk about those days now, but at the time it was painful, difficult. I was confused, hurt. What I thought looked so glamorous and fun was really dangerous and horrible. A girl in our crowd was killed one night in a car accident after a drinking party.

I have to say that even though I strayed away, Mom didn't give up on me or treat me like I was a bad person. My sister and I both flatly rebelled, but when we made decisions to give our lives back to the Lord and follow Him, she didn't say, "I told you so." I love her for that. She has never held against us the way we treated her.

The Lord restored our relationship and I was able to see her need for respect and love. I began to see her as a person, no longer the mommy she was when I was small, and not the jailor I saw her as in ninth and tenth grade, but as a person who really was good and kind, and who still was, amazingly enough, a fun person.

Now I am eighteen. This makes me a legal adult. I could move out if I wanted to. When I sign a paper, I am responsible for that signature. It's a funny feeling.

When I was fourteen I couldn't wait to be eighteen. I

figured I'd be able to shave my head, stay up all night, go out wherever I pleased, play my music as loud as I wanted to—what a picture of maturity. It's scary to think of all the adults who have no idea what fourteen-year-olds think maturity means.

When the book, *Am I the Only One Here With Faded Genes?* (Bethany House Publishers, 1987—a teen devotional I did the photography for), came out last year, I was invited along with my mother (the author) to be on radio and television interview programs to talk about it. The interviewers asked me questions like how did my mother and I become "friends," what was it like being raised in a single parent home, how does a teenage girl really feel about discipline, what are the worst problems teenage girls face today, and what message would I give today's teen? Adults really don't know those answers.

When I was a junior-high leader in the church, I had the opportunity to listen to the many complaints of girls who sounded a lot like me a few years earlier. I think I've been the most surprised, not by the girls, but by the adults and parents who don't seem to have the slightest understanding about their daughters.

The purpose of my sharing here is to talk about the daughter's side of things, because this is a book about mothers and daughters. I'll tell you, if it hadn't been for meeting so many parents of teenage girls this last year who have really been open and honest about their frustrations, and talking with so many concerned adults, I would have believed that the problem between parents and teens is probably mostly the fault of the teen. That is why I am so happy this book has been written. I needed it and my mom needed it when our relationship was hurting. We still need it—just to remind us of the hope and lasting love there for us.

I was an angry daughter, and an angry person is not a free person. Lots of teenage girls are angry. Freedom and independence, though, is a state of mind. It is an inner peace that only Jesus can give—I know that much.

I have discovered there are certain things in life I cannot angrily fight for. I can't fight for my mom's trust. I used to yell, "Mom, you just don't *trust* me!" A lot of good that did. I wanted her to respect me, so I'd shout, "Mom, when are you going to *respect* me?" A lot of good that did. She would just stand there staring at me, I suppose wondering what to say.

Some time after I made the decision to live *totally* for the Lord, I decided also to act like a trustworthy person. I decided to act like a person worthy of respect. I began to show my mother that I was responsible, honest, and that I could be true to my word. I worked hard at not demanding the right to do things my way. I learned something so valuable I hope it doesn't lose its impact here: Nothing that I want in this world is worth hurting my mom for, or breaking our communication and trust.

There are things we still disagree about—she doesn't like hard, loud music; she still has me on a curfew, she thinks I should do more work around the house than I do, and she doesn't like my baggy black coat. But she's my best friend because I want her to be, not because we're exactly alike or because either one of us is perfect. She *talks* to me, really talks—about the Lord, art (she's a terrific artist, by the way), psychology, my friends—she gives me advice on dating (and I listen)—I try to get *her* to date . . . And as I work at my drawing board and prepare for my life's work as an artist, she's there cheering me on—as my friend.

My life is not governed by my mom. It is, instead, enhanced and brightened by her. I'm proud of her. I am loyal to her. I consider my mother a friend that *I* am willing to sacrifice for. It used to be she did all the sacrificing, but now I feel I do, too. Our relationship is not pie-in-the-sky perfection. It is a lot of work and effort. Our willingness to bend is as important as is our desire to reach out for more.

We've decided we can disagree and still love each other.

She's changed, too. She gives me more space, listens, and is open. She is much more calm. My sister and I can obey her rules and respect her because it really isn't hard to do now. We know she'll bend, she'll always listen. We know she respects us and trusts us and she won't use the Bible against us. There's something more than a mother-daughter relationship between us—there's friendship and we can feel it. And maybe, if we time it just right, we can get her to be Chief Featherduster for us again and sing us funny songs about those jillions of birds in her feathers. . . .

CONTENTS

INTRODUCTION

This book explores the mother-daughter relationship, with an eye toward helping mothers and daughters discover the gift that is theirs and theirs alone. No other relationship can be compared to the one of mother and daughter; no other bond reaches the space this relationship has in the lives of females. Fathers and brothers, sisters, husbands and friends, all have their place of importance in the lives of women, and we would be hollow as drums without them, but the mother-daughter role bonds us in an inexplicable way. It may well be in fact that, until a woman separates herself from her needs, fantasies and false images of the mother and daughter roles, she will never truly see herself as a separate human being who can function as an individual in a world she longs to belong to. Perhaps it is only when a woman finds freedom from these false images and expectations that she can live the abundant life which God promises us.

Why do we daughters take on the very thoughts and drives of our mothers—even when they drive us crazy? One daughter says, "I'm becoming just like my mother. I can't stand it. All those things she did that I've always hated—like saving plastic bags, making long distance calls only after the rates go down, and trying to make everyone happy—I'm doing them now!"

In preparing this book, I talked with many mothers and daughters. I heard the heartcry of women across a span of miles and cultures, and across the span that threatens to undo these precious relationships.

A dismayed mother told me, "I always told my daughter I was perfect. Heaven help me, she *believed* me."

Another woman said, "I've never been able to distinguish myself as a person of my own. Here I am, forty years old, and sending myself to my room without dessert."

"I never had a true mother," said another. "My mom didn't want me, and she left me to raise myself. I hated her and loved her at the same time. Now I find that I'm having a problem accepting my own daughter. I almost resent it that she has a good home with parents who love and care for her, when I didn't have that."

"My mother makes me feel so guilty," said another. "I feel as if I'm always hurting her, failing her in some way. In all her life she's been so *sacrificing*. She's never eaten an undamaged cookie and was always the one who ate the burned ends of the roast. She went without a new coat so I could take ballet lessons, didn't go to the dentist so I could go to camp. I'm a horrible daughter."

One woman complained, "I can't get along with my teenager. She's an impossible person. I love her but I have to be honest—I don't like her. If I did to my mother what she does to me, I should have been struck by lightning. I don't know what to do."

I was told by one young woman, "My mother could care less about me. All she wants is her own way. She won't listen to me, won't hear me. She is just closed-minded and opinionated." And then she added, "Nothing my mother says is worth listening to."

"Perhaps the most poignant heartcry was this: "My mother died three years ago. I always was embarrassed by the way she did things, the way she talked to people, always a little too loud. . . . I didn't like her clothes or her taste in decorating. I didn't even like her job. But now I find that I'd give everything just to have her back again exactly as she was. . . ."

The feelings we keep forever can be a curse or a blessing; they depend on our mastery of communication skills, and our understanding who we are in God's eyes. Three vital points we must learn are: *first*, the skill of power prayer, a commitment to spiritual warfare; *second*, the skill of knowing and sharing goals; *third*, the skill of positive reinforcement. Developing the skill of honest, open rewarding words, shared activities and material bonuses is critical. Because people resent being "improved" or "fixed" by even those they love, we learn these three skills to bring mother and daughter together in a gratifying bond of love and friendship.

That is why it is so important to understand, and treat with tenderness, this amazing relationship.

The book includes dialogue and information for all ages, from grandmothers, to women in middle-age, to mothers with teenaged daughters or toddlers, and teenagers. There will be a special emphasis on the mother and teenaged daughter, because I have yet to see a book directed to the mother and teen daughter.

I share more in this book about my own personal life than any of the other twenty-some books I've written in the past ten years of my writing career. My daughters, Christa and Liza, who are now in their late teen years, have given me permission to write about them and our relationship, and I want to thank them for their willingness to be candid. My own mother has allowed me to write about her and about our relationship. I make no excuses for my own pursuit for her approval, and perhaps in my sharing with you my own needs as a mother, you will better understand your own— and change. I am still learning how to grow and change.

Living as mothers and daughters can be richly rewarding and an honor to God. This book is dedicated to that end.

Mankind owes to the child the best it has to give.

—*U.N. Declaration*

BRINGING UP BABY

CHAPTER ONE

Where do we begin to develop a friendship with our daughters? Is it possible to begin too soon? I don't think so. The day baby comes home is a good time to start. Or if you're a truly modern mom, you can begin the moment you give birth either in a hospital or at home when the baby is put into your safe arms and laid on your warm, welcoming body. Many mothers choose rooming-in so they are not separated from their babies after birth. Your personal circumstances and preferences will help you plan and decide how to begin this lifelong friendship—and birth is certainly just the beginning!

In this book we are focusing on becoming closer to one another, developing godly, true friendships that nothing on earth can prevail against. If your daughter is already a teenager and you're only starting to realize the relationship needs help, don't berate yourself for earlier mistakes. *Start from where you are right now.*

Let's look at those early days now, however, those days when you bring baby home for her first experiences in her new environment.

You cannot spoil a child who is under the age of eighteen

months. It is impossible to give too much love and attention to a baby. Hold your baby, carry her around with you, pick her up. Kiss her constantly.

My mother became ill after I was born and had to be rushed back to the hospital in an ambulance. The care of her first infant was placed in the hands of my grandmother. I was tightly bound in a blanket and fed a bottle every four hours. This bottle didn't reach my shrieking mouth one minute earlier than every four hours. If I shrieked too loudly, my grandmother simply closed the door. "Let the baby cry," she said, proverbially, in Norwegian, "or she will rule the home." My grandmother also wrapped woolen socks soaked in red pepper around my hands so I wouldn't suck my thumbs. That's the way they did it in the old country.

And when I became a mother years later, my grandmother told me when my first baby was born, "Now, Marie, remember not to let the baby rule the house." But I cheated. I fed my baby whenever she wanted to be fed. Sometimes twice an hour. I liked it. It was a special time between us. When she sprouted little white teeth buds, like grains of rice, I fed her biscuits to chew so she wouldn't chew on me. She was as fat as a beach ball and she was happy. So was I.

I also let her suck her thumb. (And, dear Grandma, it's amazing—she didn't get buck teeth and her thumbs aren't deformed!) My grandmother used to tell me how I sucked right through the wool and the pepper, and in Norwegian, "That child has her own mind; mark my words, she'll do as she pleases."

When I had babies of my own, they were allowed to hop and play in every room; they could sit on every chair, climb on sofas, spread their toys on the carpet (when we had one), and during the hours they were awake, they lived in "their" house. At the end of the day, all toys were put away and all was cleaned and straightened, but during the day it was a house for children. I didn't own fine furniture or anything too good for a child to roll around on. (Not always by choice.)

Today we live with lots of white—white upholstered chairs and sofas, light carpeting. (I tell my daughters it's because they no longer drool.) I can collect fragile pieces of art. I can display breakable objects. We can eat in the dining room!

I remember my grandmother as a champion at Collecting Things. She also dedicated her life to The Quest for Neatness. She collected glass objects by the millions. Every time we went to visit, my mother gave me the same solemn warning speech: "Don't run in the house; keep your hands off anything polished; don't touch anything on shelves; if it doesn't move or talk, it's not for you to play with; don't tip anything over; sit up straight and don't eat the candy in the candy dishes." The most difficult feat I accomplished as a child was not to touch everything in that wonderland of *objects d'art*, which was grandmother's house.

Next to my mother I loved my grandmother best. I learned to love her old world ways and customs as well as her love for beauty and craftsmanship. She kept a watchful eye on her irrepressible granddaughter, a child with a "mind of her own," and without her ever saying it, I knew she loved me.

The Italians and the Norwegians must agree on these child-rearing points, because the rest of the family didn't seem to disagree with my grandmother's authority on these matters. My Italian grandfather, who spoke no Norwegian, observed quietly from the edge of things, moving silently in and out of all our lives like the grand marshall of a parade.

Once when I was hopping around their living room with all its Italian and Scandinavian treasures, my grandfather rose up straight as an arrow before my grandmother, who was in hot pursuit of me, and said, "For godsake, Mattie, leave the child alone." Then he swore in Italian and the feeling I had as I slid into a corner by the damask-covered green-velvet chair with the claw feet was that of being loved.

"For godsake, Mattie, leave the child alone" told me Grandpa loved me. But then there were his brooding Sicilian glares, his unquestioning lordship over the home, the rules cast in Carrara marble. I learned that being adorable, cute, talented and bright were the most acceptable behaviors for a girl.

I had a stuffed panda bear I loved. It went everywhere with me, an ordinary stuffed animal, with the rather plain name, Johnny Panda Bear. I named him myself. One day my grandmother decided I was too old to haul around a panda bear everywhere we went. She told me in her thick Norwegian accent, "You're a big girl now, Marie, and big girls don't need teddy bears."

"Do you mean my Johnny Panda Bear?" He had one eye and only part of one arm, which was nearly worn through to the stuffing, and yet I thought he was always agreeable in spite of any personal liabilities.

My grandmother's house was an enormous hulk of a structure, perched on the side of a hill in Duluth, Minnesota. To me, Duluth was a magical city: Rome couldn't have been more exciting on its mere seven hills, for beautiful Duluth was resplendent with hills and parks right at the edge of tumultous, endless Lake Superior with its haunting foghorns, gently gliding ships and lighthouse, which I could see from my grandmother's bedroom window.

And so in that castle of a house, in those cavernous rooms, or down the wooden steps to the basement, or maybe even in the wooden garage with all the tools hung up on the wall like clothes on a line, my Johnny Panda Bear disappeared.

I searched frantically, wildly. I howled and wailed. And my grandmother said, "You're a big girl now."

I ran up and down the alley peeling lids off trash cans, calling, "Johnny?" When I became feverish, my grandmother gave me half a Bayer's aspirin and reminded my mother that children will rule the house if you don't watch out. My Johnny Bear was gone forever.

I grew up without my Johnny Panda Bear, but when I was old enough to have children of my own and they developed their loves for a scraggly bleary-eyed stuffed rabbit and a tattered, threadbare "bankee," I made these precious things part of the family. The scrawny, limp rabbit was named Bunny and had his own chair and special clothes, and Bankee was always welcome at any event or journey. We still have Bankee and Bunny, and I hope my daughters introduce them to their children when their babies fall in love with their own Panda Bears or Bunnies or Bankees, their first really true friends.

Six Bringing-Up-Baby Musts:

First, don't be afraid of spoiling your baby by picking her up too often when she cries. Your child needs to learn the feelings of security and safety. Your baby is learning a self-image even now before she can say her own name or coo "mamma" in your ear.

Second, remember that things are never as important as people. My grandmother treasured "things." Children were taught to live in her world of things. But you and I can enjoy our babies and our homes by making the place we live child-safe and child-proof. Save yourself anxiety and frustration by not buying anything white until they are old enough to sit with their feet touching the floor.

Third, a baby cries because she is in distress. It's her only means of communicating her needs to you. Go to her. Hold her. Assure her.

Fourth, be concerned with your daughter's self-image. You are the primary teacher in your daughter's life. If your child is to grow up expecting happiness, success and love with a sense of inner security and peace, you must begin to teach her now.

Fifth, give your child approval without making her feel she has to earn it. If your daughter lives with approval, she will learn to live with herself.

Sixth, make fun a part of every day. Laugh with your child, play with her. Play what she wants to play.

Research has shown that children who believe the world is a good and miraculous place and that they are special and loved have an advantage over children who are taught to be fearful and negative. Schoolteachers in the primary grades tell me children who come from punitive, non-reinforcing homes suffer with low self-value and are constantly seeking approval. These children are filled with insecurity, fear of others, fear of failure and are often dependent and unable to be loving.

A teacher pleaded with me after a seminar I once held for teachers on classroom behavior management, "Dr. Chapian, *please, please* give your message to *parents* to give to children. Tell the *mothers. . .*"

Mother, the first teacher your daughter observes is you. You're the teacher. If you let your child love the only way she knows how, you'll allow her to keep her Johnny Panda Bear until she's ready to put him on the shelf. And the same applies to little boys. "You're a big boy now" may be more frightening than encouraging.

Our calling as parents is to lead our children to the saving knowledge of Jesus Christ and to present these little ones as a pleasure to Him. Our daughters must be shown in the first stages of development that they are safe and tenderly loved. If they cry, we must be there. When they are hungry, we must provide. When they play and laugh, we should be there to play and laugh with them, showing them the world is an OK place to be and that it's a place where they are welcome.

Your friendship with your daughter begins the first time you hold her in your arms.

He who neglects discipline
despises himself,
But he who listens to reproof
acquires understanding.

—*Proverbs 15:32*

GROWING UP WITH DISCIPLINE

CHAPTER TWO

Little girls grow up. How long they're allowed to remain little girls is usually up to the parent. My grandmother told me I was a big girl now, but even months after we were back in St. Paul, I continued to look for my Johnny Panda Bear. Maybe he was in a store or in a box of old things or in a strange garbage barrel. I just didn't know enough about where panda bears might be put. Such a big world so full of corners and mysteries. Poor Johnny. Who would take care of his arm and keep it pushed back into its cottony hole? Who would explain things he couldn't see with his only eye?

The American Indians, when they were free on the plains before the white man, were a people who allowed their children to be children. Up to the age of eight, they played and were relatively irresponsible. Then, at the proper time, the boys began their serious training as young braves and warriors and the girls learned how to care for the many needs of the camp.

Many parents today hand their child a set of encyclopedias, or a doctor's stethoscope, with the admonition, "You're a big girl (boy) now. . . ." Then they are discouraged when the child prefers Mickey Mouse coloring books to *The Complete Charles Dickens*. We wag a finger in their little faces and say, "Shame, shame, you're not a *baby*, are you?" One of these days, we're going to have Ivy League preschool waiting lists for the exceptionally gifted unborn. Can you imagine the conversation of the anxious mother-to-be? ("The problem with my unborn baby is she didn't do well on the motor skills test. I just don't know what we'll do if she's not accepted at Harvard-Yale-Smith School! How will she get ahead in life?")

Samuel Butler said parents are the last people on earth who ought to have children. Let's look at the kinds of things we may fall prey to as mothers in rearing our little angels and brainy kids. (And of course *all* of us have given birth to exceptional, gifted children who owe it to us to behave perfectly so we can show them off.)

Not long ago I overheard the following speech from a mother to her little girl and I have not been able to get it out of mind. The mother, in her late twenties, was slightly overweight and dressed in a polyester wrinkle-proof pants suit and thick-soled scuffed boots. Her hair was flat against her head and pulled back behind her ears with a rubber band. The little girl standing before her, caught in the act of some "horrendous crime," had a crestfallen expression on her face, hardly matching the splendor of her appearance: white petticoats, designer dress, ruffled anklets, patent-leather Mary Jane shoes, and hair pouring down the sides of her face in massive waves and curls.

Into this sweet, dimpled face, the mother was yelling, yes *yelling*: "You may be only four years old, but you're not going to talk to your mother in that tone of voice!" She was livid. "I'm going to teach you right now who's boss here. I'm going to nip that rebelliousness right in the bud! The Bible says children are to obey their parents, and let me tell you, missy, you are going to obey me! When we get home you are going directly to your room. You can sit there all day and think about your bad behavior. I've had it with you!

You're a brat, a selfish little brat. *Go.* Just get out of my sight."

The above outburst was a real one. The mother didn't know anyone was nearby, and when I made my presence known, she broke into a broad smile, nudged her daughter to do likewise and said a cheery hello. Then, yanking the child's hand, they strutted off.

In another scene, at another time of day, this same mother may tell her child, "Why do you put yourself down like that? Don't you know Jesus loves you?" Or, "Honey, you're so special. Don't ever say 'can't.' You can do all things through Christ. Just remember there's no such thing as impossible when it comes to God."

I heard another mother scream at her three-year-old daughter not long ago, "Get away from me! Leave me alone! Just go away! You're driving me crazy. Go bug your father! I'm sick of you!" Later that same day I saw her holding the little girl in her arms and telling her how precious she was.

What are the messages of life and love these children are learning in their tender early years? Are they getting mixed messages, like those I've mentioned? Are they learning that they are tyrants and monsters wreaking havoc in an otherwise peaceful adult world? And at the same time, are they hearing that they are adorable and Jesus loves them, for the Bible tells them so?

Margaret Mead, the famed sociologist, once said, while conducting her penetrating studies of families in primitive societies around the world, "We must have . . . a place where children can have a whole group of adults they can trust."

When I was a little girl I learned that being adorable, cute, talented and bright were acceptable behaviors. When I think about it now, I think I always had a sense of being (for lack of a better word for it) entertaining.

My bond to my mother was intensely strong. I cannot remember her ever being genuinely angry with me. Her method of punishment was to sit me in the corner on her cedar chest. This punishment I accepted with some of the finest dramatic performances of my career.

In all the years of growing up with my mother, I do not recall ever seeing her face red with rage or her temper flared to the point of erupting with a raised, irate voice. (I wish my daughters could say the same.) Even as a teenager, when I thought of myself as a star swimmer—English Channel material—and I would swim across our northern Minnesota lakes daily, I'd be halfway to the other side when I'd hear my mother calling from the shore behind me: "Mar—ieee, Mar—ieee, come baaack, come baaack!" I'd swim on, ignoring her command. After reaching my destination and flapping homeward through the water, I'd see her outline on our dock. When I stroked nearer, it wasn't rage and indignation I was met with, but a towel.

My mother was my friend. She wasn't from the same world as my grandmother, in whose life Perfect Order existed and everything was precise, exquisite and untouchable. When I talked to my mother she listened, as though what I had to say was interesting. I made her laugh. She didn't insist that I be a big girl. When I cried, she held me. Later she taught me about beauty and exercise. She encouraged my dreams for a better future. She helped me, defended me, trusted me and I always felt (and still do) that she genuinely believed in me.

When I was an infant, my mother held the keys to life and happiness. She was the miracle worker, the heroine of the hour at all times. She could open a cupboard and magically make a shelf of things appear.

It's the mother who transports the child to new worlds as she moves from room to room, as she takes her child outside, feeds her, clothes, bathes her, talks to her, reads to her, holds her, loves her.

Some mothers expect the father to be the disciplinarian, if there is to be one in the family at all. It was my father who disciplined me. He taught me the "wages of sin is death," let me tell you. My feelings toward my father could be put in a single word: fear. And this fear led to my overt efforts to earn his approval. I wasn't always successful, but I learned young that the way to get people to love you is to do and act exactly as they want.

Just this past spring I was out with a group of people in a restaurant and one of the women had brought her five-year-old daughter along. The little girl, who needed to feel cute and who evidently had a strong need for approval, ran from one of us to the other, throwing her arms around our necks and whispering sweetly in our ears, "I love you!" We all appropriately responded, "I love you, too, dear." The child was satisfied.

Behavior such as this may be acceptable for the five-year-old, but it is not suitable for an adult. Sometimes, when grown-up daughters have a need for approval and a strong desire to feel cute, we're left with few options. How to have our needs fulfilled, that is the question. There we are, boxed in between the bills, the laundry, the dentist appointments, the long hours of work and the gang of kids in the family room who think most parents are out of it. If you're standing alone in the kitchen with your broom in one hand and the dustpan in the other, with a deep need for acceptance and a sense of being feminine and "cute," God help you.

So where does Mother go to have her needs fulfilled? What does she do? She can turn to her husband, if she's blessed to have one who responds well to her needs. She can say, "Honey, will you please tell me you love me? I need to hear that right now."

She can run from one person to another, throwing her arms around them, whispering "I love you" in hopes of hearing a genuine "I love you, too, dear" in return. But this is iffy, at best.

As children, we learned that "adorable" or "cute" earns approval. We learned that obedience earns approval, like the little girl I told you about at the beginning of this chapter. So we have millions of women running around being cute and obedient. A regular generation of Stepford Wives.

Maria Montessori said, "The first idea that the child must acquire, in order to be actively disciplined, is that of the difference between good and evil; and the task of the educator lies in seeing that the child does not confound good with immobility, and evil with activity."

We learned as little girls that being quiet and sitting still was "good behavior." Instead of learning that some behaviors are inappropriate and undesirable, we mistake the discipline to mean we are bad. Therefore, if we made loud noises, ran indoors, got our dresses muddy, yelled at our baby brother, talked out loud in church, touched Grandma's blown-glass pelican, we were bad. Maria Montessori continues, ". . . Our aim is to discipline for activity, for work, for good; not for immobility, not for passivity."

When the Lord disciplines us, it is not out of an ego need. Ps.94:12 says: "*Blessed* is the man whom Thou dost chasten, O Lord, and dost teach out of Thy law."

There are many books written to the Christian parent on how to spare the rod and spoil the child. Love cannot be without discipline, and we are responsible to teach our children how to live within the laws of God, obeying Him with our whole hearts. The purpose of this chapter is to encourage us as mothers (and daughters) to understand the difference between *earning* approval and obeying the Lord by living in the power of the Word of God.

Mothers, how do we make it in a world that keeps trying to mess up our lovableness? The mother I told you about, the one who was screaming at her daughter to get lost and leave her alone, could have used a big dose of assurance that she was OK, her world was OK, and life was not going to do her in. The mother who uses the Bible as a butcher block can use a big dose of the assurance of God's loving protection and concern for His own. When we're not so adorable, we somehow believe—I mean, we really believe—that we're no longer lovable; therefore we don't qualify for the sweetness of God in our lives.

My daughters, who are still in their teen years, tell me they want to be independent. They want to be free of parental restrictions. They want to spread their wings and fly—taste the nectar of experience and eat of the banquet of life. I want to tell them to have a glass of lemonade and light the hibachi, and as for flying they can always get on a plane and go visit Grandma.

I have this sneaky urge to *control* their lives, to insist they do things the way I am quite sure they should be done.

First off, topping the list as *primero numero uno* is: Don't Leave Mama Because Mama Needs Your Acceptance and Love. OK, so I allowed them to be little girls for as long as they wanted to be; I didn't send them to the preschool for the Future Leaders of the World; I didn't take away their Bankee and their Bunny, or demand they take their thumbs out of their mouths when company was around. But does that mean I now have to let them go, fly away, *leave me?*

Wanting to spread one's wings is normal for a girl, and I don't want to obstruct the normal growth process. I want the best for my children. I have often joked (but only partially) that when they get married, I come with the package. I've thought about drawing up an agreement that the lucky, privileged guy who lands one of these prized daughters will have to sign before betrothal. It will state that he will never take the girls farther than five miles from their mom.

Nobody prepares us for saying goodbye to our children. There's a plethora of books and material on how to say hello; the card catalogs at the library are swollen with titles of books for the pregnant woman and the parent of the newborn. But how about the day you must say and mean it to your girl, "You're a big girl now. Goodbye"?

What then?

Then you will know that your daughter has learned that

discipline is happiness and it is wisdom and self-esteem (see Prov. 15:31, 32). You will have taught your daughters, ". . . happy is the [woman] whom God reproves, so do not despise the discipline of the Almighty" (Job 5:17). You will know when your daughter is ready to discipline herself in a world away from you by watching her discipline herself at home.

Someone once said there are only two lasting bequests we can hope to give our children. One of these is roots; the other, wings.

When your child flies, so do you.

I feel guilty if I don't put everyone else's needs before my own. I believe in being unselfish and giving, and yet I can't ever seem to do enough. I can't seem to make other people happy enough. And I don't feel satisfied even when I am doing for others. So I feel even more guilty. I feel I don't deserve the love people show me. I haven't really earned it.

—A Thirty-Year-Old Christian Woman

MOTHER GUILT

CHAPTER THREE

Women know that one of the most fundamental functions of being a woman is to nurture others. Becoming a mother multiplies this urge. Sociologist Jessie Bernard said, "Motherhood is more than the biological process of reproduction. It is an institution consisting of customs, traditions, conventions, beliefs, attitudes, mores, rules, laws, precepts, and the host of other rational and nonrational norms that deal with the care and rearing of children."[1]

I've seen the Christian mother's sense of duty to nurture and give selflessly become an obsessive-compulsive behavior pattern. Instead of helping and comforting others, she can irritate and condemn them.

Eugene Peterson wrote, "A parent's main job is not to be a parent, but to be a person."[2] This is a difficult concept for us when we're so sold on the idea that living selflessly gives us the right to maintain a dictatorship. And what is the main tool to keep the dictatorship in top form? Guilt.

Sacrifice on the mother's part usually means guilt on the

---

[1]Jessie Bernard, *The Future of Motherhoood* (New York: Dial Press, 1971).
[2]Eugene Peterson, *Growing Up in Christ: A Guide for Families With Adolescents* (Atlanta: John Knox Press, 1976).

daughter's part. If we mothers are to engage in sacrificial giving, it begins with sacrificing our strong drives to *control.* Sacrificing means to vow to stop using guilt as a rod of correcting.

Guilt is a monster.

Of all the pain of child-rearing, guilt may be one of the top offenders.

What we tell ourselves about being mothers affects our self-esteem right down to the nub. If I tell myself, "I'm less than what a mom should be because I don't fit the traditional parent mold," my behavior is going to follow suit. Let's look at the following description of "the mold":

> I am first and foremost a mother. The commitment to my children is forever. I am responsible for their overall care— physical and emotional. I am on call for their needs twenty-four hours a day.[3]

Many of us assume that if we do not agree with the above statement and fulfill it in every act, thought and deed throughout the day from baking cookies, to car-pooling, to buying educational materials, to nursing, to supervising free time, to volunteering in school, to music and dancing lessons, to buying good clothes and keeping clothes mended and pressed, to helping with homework to typing papers, to outdoing other mothers, to having meals on time with all the basic food groups, to doing science projects, to having regular family devotions and prayer time without fail—if we fail in any of this, we are guilty.

A girlfriend of mine, a pastor's wife, was at my house for a prayer meeting one afternoon when the phone rang. It was her husband. I heard my friend say into the telephone, "You're hungry?—Well, I'll be home in a little bit. Oh, OK—no, it won't be long. I'll leave right now."

She hung up and sighed, with a resigned expression on

---

[3]Marjorie Hanson Shaenitz, *The Superwoman Syndrome* (New York: Warner Books, 1984).

her face. "He's hungry," she said.

My imagination swept me away. I couldn't figure out why this grown man, leader of an entire church, couldn't open a cupboard door by himself. I asked her, "Do you hide the refrigerator out in the trees where nobody can find it?" "Oh, you know how men are," she replied, smiling wanly. "So helpless without us women." But her excuse was as empty as the look in her eye.

A week later when she was visiting me again, her twelve-year-old daughter called. My friend grimaced into the receiver and said, "Well, honey, I can't come home right now. Why don't you just wait until I get home and then I'll make you something to eat." Her daughter was hungry and wanted Mom to come home and feed her. This able-bodied child, who was taking computer science in school and playing Bach etudes on the piano, couldn't wash an apple for herself.

We create helpless wimps out of the people we love because of our own guilt urges. We tell ourselves, "If I'm not putting the needs of others before my own, I feel guilty." This is a ridiculous practice.

The working mom can be a walking guilt bomb and so can the single mother (whom we'll talk about in the next chapter). She feels if she is not a full-time mother at home or is without a spouse to bring home the bacon, she is less than a *real* mom. She's not *traditional*.

Dr. Ray Guarendi tells us the two-parent, mom-stays-home and dad-goes-to-work arrangement, "while it may sound as American as apple pie, actually describes less than twenty-five percent of the parenting configurations in our country today."[4]

Dr. Guarendi goes on to say that the parents in the majority—including step-parents, biological parents not living

⁴Ray Guarendi, *You're a Better Parent Than You Think* (New York: Prentiss-Hall, 1985).

full time with their children, single, adoptive or foster parents, working mothers, and any combination thereof—have a common, demoralizing habit. They strip legitimacy from their own parenting roles by convincing themselves that they are not the standard. "They draw the demeaning conclusion that since they are 'nontraditional' parents, they are less than deserving of a full measure of parental authority and rights."[5]

The paradox here is that, without realizing, accepting and implementing the full measure of parental authority, mothers of today are much less effective with their children. If a mother chips away at her rights and responsibilities through doubting her status as a qualified mother, her confidence and parental mental health suffers considerably.[6]

Back in 1976, a book appeared called *Working Mothers*, written by a woman named Jean Curtis. In those days, Dr. Spock was hailed as supreme guru to mothers. His book *Baby and Child Care* was first published in 1946, and women of the seventies were still carrying it in their diaper bags. His book *Raising Children in a Difficult Time* was published in 1974, but parents were questioning the venerable doctor's counsel and some even dared call his advice hollow.

Listen to this: Dr. Spock wrote in his 1974 book that a father, during the hours when he is at home, "should take part in the care of his child." He adds, "We have to face the fact, however, that there are still millions of fathers today who have not participated much in the care of their children. . . . The first question is whether the children will suffer as a consequence of this lack of relationship. *Not necessarily.* A child can admire and gain inspiration from a father who is so dignified, or so unhandy at making things, or so uninterested in sports and nature that he can't enjoyably do any of these things, if father and child are reasonably

---

[5]Ibid.
[6]Ibid.

comfortable with each other and can talk spontaneously at the dinner table from time to time."

Ms. Curtis raises the question, "At what point does a mother's need for reliable, committed participation in the parenting process take precedence over the quaintness of fatherly helplessness?" She adds that there has never been anything quaint about a *mother* who can't change diapers, cook three meals a day, keep a clean and orderly house, administer to the emotional needs of her family and find time, in odd moments, to explore her own private initiatives, professional or otherwise. Research shows that fathers who share the parenting responsibilities more equally wish they'd done so from the beginning.

Parents are now in circumstances that make it necessary for Mother to work outside the home; and amazingly, women are yet caring intimately for their babies, bonding longer, and enjoying their lives. Marriages are intact and children are happy. Dr. Spock's portrait of the dignified, unhandy father sitting tacitly and authoritatively at the dinner table is an unhappy one, and by Christian standards, maladjusted.

Wives, as well as husbands, are realizing that a lot of their ideas and feelings about parenting have been based on myth and poor advice. True, disturbed relationships are to be found in families where the mother works, but there is equal evidence that disturbed family relationships abound in homes where only one parent, usually the father, is working.

Spockian authors tell mothers how to handle a baby herself, but she is not informed how to speak to the day-care teacher, the housekeeper, the live-in baby-sitter, or the play-group leader—or even her husband.

Elizabeth Janeway said, "Closed minds accept myth most easily, but a frightened society seeks it actively."[7] Guilt

---

[7]Elizabeth Janeway, *Man's World, Woman's Place* (New York: Morrow, 1971).

must be examined. We accept it too easily. God did not intend for guilt to be a controlling force in our lives. He meant it to be an agent for cleansing and renewal.

The fears we have must be examined, too. We accept fear too easily. Women raise children to be helpless, dependent people and then they instill guilt into their children for not being grateful for their condition. When we motivate by guilt, we succeed in motivating the people we love to be helpless and dependent, at least to *us*. To the rest of the world they may be capable and even self-sufficient, but once around Mom, they are transformed into helpless bumpkins whining about nothing to eat in the refrigerator and no clean socks to wear. The problem this mother faces every day of her life is how to feel important. How does she find her sense of value?

We may point at the female executive, warning her of living "in the flesh" with her worldly pursuits for success in the business world. But we cannot overlook the fact that there are many manipulating mothers whose desperate unmet needs to feel important are producing spoiled, self-seeking children and husbands. The sad part of it is, we smile with approval because of appearances, not facts.

"Did you know Cynthia bakes her own bread from scratch and sews all her daughters clothes?" This kind of statement can receive oohs and ahhs, but nobody asks about Cynthia's short temper. And nobody asks why everybody feels so guilty and defensive at Cynthia's house.

When I show my daughter a sunrise, perfect and splendid, I want it to be something we share, a moment arrested, as in a photograph to keep in our hearts.

In romantic love between a man and a woman, dependency does not contribute to godliness and, as Eric Fromme puts it, "fusion with integrity."[8] Saint-Exupery said, "Love does not consist in gazing at each other [one perfect sunrise

---

[8]Marie Chapian, *Growing Closer* (New Jersey: Revell, 1985).

gazing at another!] but in looking outward together in the same direction."

Can we give the view that we gaze upon to our daughters—without guilt?

*When my anxious thoughts
multiply within me, Thy
consolations delight my soul.*

—*Psalm 94:19*

THE SINGLE MOTHER

CHAPTER FOUR

When I was a young wife and my children were babies, I remember thinking I had everything I would ever want in life. I was completely happy with the sweetness of the world I believed was mine. We lived in New York City, and though we didn't have much money, our lives, I believed, were rich with love. We later moved to Minnesota where trees grow freely and there is enough sky for everybody, and it was not hard to say goodbye to the big city.

But I had much to learn about the word goodbye.

I had given up a career in the theatre to be a wife and mother, and I had never regretted the decision. Some goodbyes are not difficult to make because of the promises of happier hellos. But, as I said, I had much to learn about the word goodbye.

I remember a picture; it is forever snapped in my brain like a scrapbook entry: There stood my two little girls when they were five and six, so tiny and thin . . . one with flaxen hair and green eyes like her mamma and the other brown eyed and dark haired like her daddy—fragile, sweet little girls. . . .

There were trees outside our windows and we had a

screen door and a lilac bush. It was spring and the world was a thick, lilac-perfumed green. Two little girls by the side of the house were softly, noiselessly crying.

I saw the little one, blond hair in two pigtails at the sides of her head, start to run after her daddy, past the screen door, down the long driveway on the hill; and the other girl, face screwed up and pinched, rubbing her eyes and slumped on the steps. Then both girls, so small against the wood siding of the suburban house on a hill where all the nice folk live, watched in silence as their daddy left without looking back.

The screen door had snapped shut, nothing moved, but the lilacs by the kitchen window bloomed and filled the air with impertinent sweetness. We watched him leave for the last time, heard the car engine fade. A bee fumbled at the lilacs.

Our little world was no more. Daddy was gone.

My daughters missed their father, as I did. For days after, Christa cried. She held on to my arm with her tiny hands and asked, "Why, Mommy? Why did Daddy leave us? We're good Christians, aren't we?"

I didn't think I would ever recover from that moment. A part of something living and breathing fell out of my body, a part of my heart. Her face, her little face with those luminous eyes looking up at me, begging for an answer as to why bad things happen to good people.

I wasn't strong enough to handle this moment, not big enough. I was just a good Christian, a nice person, a simple person. What did I know about handling such gigantic problems, such grief and anguish? These two tiny people: How could I, the Loser of the Universe, be any good to them?

There are times in our lives that dig talons into our minds, like wild beasts, hungry for our sanity. I remember those days very well, when I struggled to piece our lives together. I still bear some emotional scars: shyness, fear of rejection—like a person with broken bones who walks forever with a limp.

Having felt so loved, I suddenly felt completely unlovable. I knew I was acceptable in the Christian world as a wife and mother—but as a single mother, that was a different story. Friendships terrified me. (Confessing my insecurities, even now, is difficult for me to do.) I would like to tell you that all I did was cast my cares upon Him and *presto*, I was healed, but it would not be true. I cast and I cast, but I fumbled and I bumbled.

Today, more than a few years later, I face new challenges and new problems, though I don't feel I'm limping painfully and fretfully onward through each trial. There came a day when I chose to stop fumbling and bumbling. I've learned to hurt with dignity. Learned the integrity of the soul's struggle for value. Satan robs us of our human worth and Jesus died on the cross to give it back. He died to give us life.

Self-pity is without dignity; it's like death. Feelings of self-hatred and inferiority are like death, too. Joylessness robs us of life. I feel as if I have risen, as Lazarus did, from the tomb. And like Lazarus I have come forth. Grave clothes and all.

I hobbled out of my sadness at the sound of the Master's voice. "I am come to give you life. . . ."

It's magnificent to hear the call of the Lord, to take His offer of life abundant—to keep it.

When I think of Jesus raising Lazarus from the dead, I wonder if Lazarus suffered any aftereffects, like stiff knees, or poor circulation, or digestive troubles. I felt I was raised up whole.

One thing I am certain of, and that is that after being raised from the dead, Lazarus had to find it impossible to complain. And I am confident he was never again afraid. How can you doubt God when you've been raised from a stinking corpse to a living, breathing person again?

I am a Lazarus. Jesus called, "Come forth, Marie," and grave clothes and all, I stumbled out of the cave of death into the light of himself. It was nothing short of a miracle to become disentangled from self-pity, fear, worry, hurt, sorrow, loneliness, my grave clothes. How can I ever complain again? I'm alive, I'm free. I'm no longer buried in grief.

That feeling of being left alone to rot was very real to me. My heart goes out to every woman who experiences such feelings of loss and rejection, whether it be by divorce or death of a loved one.

Redemption is what I needed. I found divine relief, freedom from the crushing, vicious demons of self-hate. Freedom in the redeeming power of Jesus Christ.

Redemption. I love that word. We Christians are redeemed from our own personal hells.

Here's what I did: I began a daily program of personal Bible study to learn what God had to say about me and my situation. Did He see me as defeated and helpless, a person without hope? Did He reject me, too? Was my life and ministry over? Would my life ever count for anything again? Was I a terrible person? What about my little girls? Surely God wouldn't reject them, would He? Why would God hurt and punish us like this?

The Lord showed me through searching the Scriptures that He had given me everything I would ever need in this life to live out His will for me. Even in trial and despair, I lacked nothing. In suffering and sorrow, I lacked nothing. In heartache, hunger, poverty or sickness, I lacked nothing. God had given His Son for me, and His Spirit dwelled in me. I lacked nothing.

I realized my life was meant for one purpose and one purpose only: to glorify the Lord. I was called to please God, to bring Him pleasure, to glorify Him. I felt unworthy and uncertain if God's heart was open to me at all, and so I asked Him one day, "If you are a God of love, why is my interpretation of love so different?" And it was then I understood how much of my understanding about God was based on my understanding of human behavior and human feelings.

No human being can say, "My grace is sufficient for you" when a loved one needs a thorn removed. No human being can say, "I will never leave you nor forsake you."

I couldn't go on without allowing the Holy Spirit within me to ignite my faith by God's Word. I devoured the Word, literally. I was determined to rise up as His person, no matter how battered, to become totally fueled and motivated by the fire of His Spirit. Even if I was a factory reject, a loser, it became my passion to discover God's mind in things. God, after all, had said love was His name. *God is love*—what did He mean by that?

I focused on scriptures where God spoke of himself, His heart toward us, His goals for us. I paraphrased, personalized and spoke these scriptures out loud to myself. I repeated over and over again, "His grace is sufficient for me. His grace is sufficient for me."

I repeated out loud, "I am casting my burdens on the Lord; I am releasing the weight of my burdens on the Lord because He says He will sustain me. He said He will never allow me to be moved—to slip, fall or fail. . ." (Ps. 55:22).

I repeated out loud, "The Lord God is a sun and shield; the Lord gives grace and favor and glory—No good thing will He withhold from those who walk uprightly. . ." (Ps. 84:11).

"Happy, fortunate, to be envied is the person who trusts in the Lord. . . . Happy, fortunate, to be envied is the person who leans on and believes in you, Lord, committing all and confidently looking to you. I will be without fear!" (Ps. 84:12).

"He has loved me with an everlasting love . . . with loving kindness He has drawn me. . ." (Jer. 31:3).

Over and over again, hundreds of times a day I spoke the precious words of truth out loud to myself. I realized how dead in grief and shame I had become and how in need of a spiritual resurrection I was. Gloriously and gradually it happened.

My Lazarus experience. There came a day when I knew I was all right, when I knew God's grace *was* sufficient for me—when I could truly accept Him as my sun and shield—when my arms and heart became expectantly open to His grace and favor and glory—when I knew I would wholeheartedly receive all that lay ahead, rough or smooth, because it was well with my soul; I was happy, fortunate and to be envied. I was loved with an everlasting love and I wholly trusted God. I could come out of the tomb now. I was alive.

How holy and sublime to be able to sing aloud, "I'm *alive*, redeemed by the blood of the Lamb; I'm free to live, to soar, to love, to dance, to breathe, to laugh, to learn, to grow, to draw pictures in the sand, to look straight into the face of an innocent-eyed child and proclaim, "I will lift up mine eyes unto the hills, from whence cometh my help. My help cometh from the Lord, which made heaven and earth."

Skills of the Single Mom

I have met and known several single mothers and they all share at least one common trait worth discussing here: guilt. Motherhood is a stressful job even when there is a father on the scene. A single mother with no husband or father in the home has double stress. Total all of the stresses of parenting and multiply them by two for each child you have and you'll come up with the approximate stress level you live with daily as a single mother. I tell you this so you will learn to recognize mothering fallacies. You do not have a partner to remind you of parenting fallacies and unrealistic demands upon you to be the Perfect Mother, so you must do it yourself.

Here are some false beliefs that induce guilt in the single mother:

• I am personally to blame for my daughter's problems.

- I am a bad person because I have no husband.
- I am to blame for my daughter's insecurity.
- I am at fault for our poor financial situation.
- If I were a better person, I'd be able to give my daughter a decent father.
- I'm not a good mother.
- I'm terrible at discipline and I lose my temper and so I'm probably doing harm to my daughter's psyche.
- I've ruined my daughter's chance for happiness and success.

Believing yourself to be an inadequate person, you will devalue yourself as a woman and as a mother. You'll seek ways to atone for your inadequacy. One way is to be lax and place only limited and weak requirements upon your children. It will be your way of saying, "Since I deprived you of your father—which I'm sure will cause you irreparable pain and damage—I'll make it up to you by making your life as easy as possible."

Self-reproach is a way of life for most single mothers. A popular misbelief is: "I was a failure at marriage; I'm probably going to be a failure at mothering, too." So the single mother fearfully imposes rules as though they were red-hot irons, too hot to handle. Daily tasks like taking out the garbage, cleaning the bathtub, or feeding the dog become monumental. Asking the daughter to do so much as one easy load of laundry can arouse such guilt it's not worth asking. The attitude is this: "Oh, you poor kid, you're from a broken home. Just sit there and watch TV. I'll do the dishes." And while you're mopping the spaghetti-stained dishes, you're gazing over at your fatherless waif who sits blank-eyed before the TV set and you silently bemoan her tragic fate in life.

Self-blame is a killer and its chief characteristics are false beliefs. For example, one shouldn't always assume two parents in the house are always better than one. A loving, intelligent, happy well-adjusted husband and wife, yes, but just the number two in itself is no magic formula.

You say you know all this. The divorce wasn't your choice after all. You got married for keeps, and who would have guessed you'd wind up in this predicament. Besides, there are no good, eligible Christian guys out there, and your poor kids have to go through life without a dad. Or if they do have a dad, he's only around on weekends and he's either a real lout or he's a great guy you just can't happen to live with. Worse, he's remarried and blissfully happy, and you feel he ignores the kids.

So the suffering single mother punishes herself one notch further on the torture rack. She sacrifices all for her deprived little ones. She caters to her poor darlings to the point where they're wearing designer clothes, carrying designer book bags, going to the orthodontist, the optometrist, the dermatologist, the psychologist, and Mom is sitting home in the same clothes she wore in high school and having all her serious operations done at home (by the Welcome Wagon lady).

In order to assuage the guilt, the relationship between mother and daughter takes on this dynamic: "I give—you take; you demand—I comply."

More than four million people in the United States are raising children without full-time spouses. That means at this moment four million people are dealing with the desire to "make it up" to their children. It's important to face this tendency head-on and examine your own faulty beliefs about single-parenting. It is true that life is not fair. Some of us have handicaps we're forced to live with—physical, emotional, intellectual, financial and situational.

And there's *no way* you can make it up to your daughter. Tell yourself the truth now, with these "I can'ts":

- I can't remove the pain of life for my daughter.
- I can't make the bad go away all the time.

- I can't shield my daughter from sorrow and hurt.
- I can't re-do the past.

Now tell yourself the following "I can's":

- I can share a fun, happy home with my daughter in spite of our situation.
- I can stop thinking of our home as "broken."
- I can give my daughter support and positive reinforcement.
- I can read books, attend seminars, classes and groups for single parents, and fellowship with other single mothers to provide myself with a positive support system.
- I can worship God, study the Bible and pray with my daughter and experience the power and faithfulness of the Lord with her as a family.
- I can provide strong family traditions and instill family pride in our family *exactly as it is* instead of treating our family as a poor, underprivileged one waiting for a rescuer.
- I can give my daughter a loving, happy, creative mom who makes the best of every situation I encounter.
- I can show my daughter the glory of trusting God in all things by my own life, and trust in the One who loves our family as we are.
- I can dare to impose rules and regulations because it is good for both of us to live with boundaries, rules and deadlines.
- Our family is a loving one and requires all of our participation; therefore, we each have jobs to do and tasks to complete on time. I am not afraid to insist upon this.
- I can explain consequences of noncompliance to rules and jobs and enforce this punishment without guilt.
- I can see myself as a beautiful person even though I

do not have a spouse to tell me I am beautiful.
- I can allow my daughter to be young, and I will not expect her to comfort me as my source of social reinforcement. I will not expect her to take the place of an adult in my life.
- I will make friends who are uplifting and encouraging.
- I will set goals for myself academically as well as career-wise.
- I will not feel guilty when I have to take my daughter to the baby-sitter or to day care. I will pride myself on choosing the best care I can find. If it ever appears to me to be less than the best, I will change it.
- My daughter is not a helpless waif. I am there for her, as a parent ought to be. I do not have to sacrifice my life and health for her in order to do penance for the fact that she does not have a father in the house. I can think of my daughter as a healthy, normal and capable person.
- I can stop seeing my daughter as an unwanted loser for whose horrible lot in life I am to blame.
- I can stop thinking of myself as "poor," even if we are on welfare. I can start valuing the riches of a life in Christ and seeing us as a family who can find something wonderful even in the smallest things.
- I can start building wonderful, happy memories for my daughter by creating hobbies and activities we do together regularly.

Single mothers battle with the desire to overcompensate for the absence of a father. Many times this is an emotional rather than rational investment. She will spoil her daughter with unhealthy foods and sweets, late-night television, lack of discipline, but she won't invest in furthering her own education to prepare her for a job that could allow her to send her daughter to a good, private Christian school.
One woman told me, "I am sending my children to a

private Christian school, and I have yet to meet another single mother among the parents. Other single mothers either don't want to fork out the money for a private school education or they don't have it. All I know is, for all those Christmas, Easter, spring, summer, Halloween and special programs, recitals, plays, musicals, and graduations, I sit alone in an audience half-full of daddies."

Another Christian single mom told me, "When my kids have new friends from the church over, they always ask, 'Where's your dad?' When the Sunday-school teachers call, they ask for "Mr.," and when the fall father-daughter banquets are held, I always feel absolutely terrible for my girl. That's when it's hardest to keep face."

A single mom of two teenaged boys told me, "The boys and I attend a church where over half the church membership is made up of single people, yet the pastor doesn't seem to be aware of it. He delivers his messages to a married congregation. When he speaks to men, he addresses them as "husbands," and almost all of his sermon illustrations are about his own wife and kids. How can we relate?"

She went on to tell me, "There is no singles fellowship in the church and no counseling provided for divorced or widowed people. We're usually treated as the 'wounded' or the 'unfortunate.'

"Because of the lack of a singles fellowship, I missed out on some crucial support and friendship when I needed it most. The church simply didn't have the help and encouragement I needed. It still doesn't, but I've learned to live with it."

This is a sad commentary on an all-too-common attitude in many churches. Many pastors believe the most important message singles need to hear is to abstain from evil, to beware of lust, and to avoid fleshly indulgences. My daughters told me that at their Christian school in junior high, every guest speaker spoke on one of three things: sex, drugs or evil music. As though the pre-teen has nothing else on his or her mind.

So groups and sub-groups of people are stereotyped. The married mother is pictured as glued to her kitchen stove and laundry basket when she is not at her aerobics class. The single mother is thought of as wanton and needy and filling her lonely hours with wild singles events. Single women are expected to be desperate for a man, just as single men are thought of as somehow incomplete if they are not married. Single people are not helpless if the Holy Spirit enriches and floods the heart with himself.

It is vital for the single mother to stop fulfilling the Wounded Helpless Female stereotype and begin to see the power she has in Christ.

Some single mothers, because they have accepted the stereotypes, choose to stay on welfare even after the kids are in school instead of furthering their own education and setting their sights on a gratifying career or job. Others have frozen self-images that keep them bound to unsatisfying lifestyles.

If you are a single mom, you must see yourself as a competent, achieving person with dynamic potential to contribute to this world. Stop giving up and living life on "hold" while you wait for a man.

No amount of trouble, pain, sorrow, illness, financial distress and loneliness can remove us from the tight, loving grip of God. Again and again, I thank Him for being the Father to the fatherless, Lord of Lords, and Savior to all mothers who constantly need reminding that none of us who call ourselves Christian are single-handed.

Our children are His children first.

I hear and I forget. I see and I remember. I do and I understand.

—*Chinese Proverb*

WHAT ARE WE TEACHING
OUR DAUGHTERS?

CHAPTER FIVE

Can you describe your spiritual vision of yourself? In showing your daughter the Perfect Sunrise, how do you explain it? There you are, "looking outward." You're somebody's daughter and you're somebody's mother. Who are you?

> Parent,
> daughter,
> person?

Is it all one and the same?

It's a sad reality that some Christian women tend to be more helpless than women who don't even know the Lord. We aren't really sure *who* we are.

We women of God, to whom the Lord gives strength and power and dignity, live like weak, ineffectual children who need others to affirm our personhood constantly.

Sometimes, our trust in the Lord is sub-zero. We panic about growing old. We see ourselves only in terms of today, right now, this hour. We sabotage ourselves as mothers, females and Christians when we fail to put being *Christian* first in our lives. If we don't find our personhood in Jesus Christ, we'll always be desperately prowling the world looking for someone else to heal us and make the bad go away.

The Christian mom can be a *dependent* woman, so busy playing out her role as a needy child that she never really taps the kingdom resources available to her in Christ. Living in a two-parent household is no assurance of parental wisdom and confidence. The mother in this ideal situation could have dependency needs outweighing those of her children! "Daddy is daddy of us all" is the household theme. "Daddy will tell us what to do. He'll rescue us. He'll fix things. He'll feed us, clothe us, give us money for toys and fun things."

But when this woman doesn't meet Daddy's expectations, she's infused with guilt. She feels as though she is inadequate and inept as a woman and a wife. She also pouts and cries when she doesn't get her way, thereby teaching her daughters there is no difference between a little girl and a grown-up, except that you get taller, a fuller body, and more privileges.

Tragically, while we're scratching the crust of life begging for attention, we may have a small person at our knee, looking to us for a feeling of safety and security and a vision of womanhood.

A second type woman is the *dominant* woman who essentially directs the lives of the family. She demands perfection of herself and runs her house like a well-greased machine. She has high expectations of herself as a mother and wife, which she pursues with deepest dedication. The flaw in this scenario is that if the children fail or go wrong, she takes it so personally that it nearly does her in. In Chapter Eleven, we'll take a closer look at this type of woman when we meet a woman named Elaine.

The dominant woman needs to learn to release her drive to control to the Lord Jesus, whether she is controlling by doing everything "right" or by remaining weak and helpless. Daily, moment-by-moment if necessary, these controls must be given over to the One who can bring order and beauty to her life.

For example, there is the mother who insists her daughter study, study, study. She teaches her from the first day of nursery school that success and being the best are all-important. But one day the daughter pauses in her competitive race and looks at her own mother's life. Her mother graduated from a good college with honors, succeeded at marrying an ambitious professional man, and today she lives in a big house with a pool, a maid, three dogs and two kids.

This same mother is hassled, constantly complaining, always on a diet and worried about losing her looks. If this is a successful woman, who wants it?

A third type of mother is the one who *nags* her daughter to pretty up, do something with herself, wear makeup, lose weight, straighten her skirt, take ballet, smile more, develop a charming, phony personality—all for one important purpose: to meet Mr. Right one day and marry him.

"Just remember, honey," this mother warns her daughter, "until you're married, you're just one man away from welfare."

Mom herself is living proof of this advice. She married the most handsome, promising guy on her college campus and she did it with her charm, her good looks and her terrific personality. Mom always watched her weight, hung her clothes up when she took them off, bathed regularly, never wore scruffy old tennis shoes—and for what?

Today she's haggard, nervous, and Mr. Right is on the road two weeks out of every month. Mom, for all her prettiness and charm, sits in front of the television set seven nights a week drinking wine out of a coffee mug. She rarely laughs, and the only reading material she buys are cheap romance novels and Hollywood gossip tabloids.

Another type of mother is the one who teaches her daughters that without money the quality of life is positively defiled. And the only way to make money or marry money, these mothers believe, is to get an education. So the daughters look at their mothers who are strung out, hung up,

undone, burned out, stressed out, wiped out, but *educated*.
And the daughters ask, "Why? What's it all for?" Sylvester
Stalone didn't go to college, Mom. Madonna didn't go to
college and she's one of the richest women around. And look
at Liz Taylor—she's wearing jewelry that belonged to the
Duchess of Windsor. Did she graduate from high school,
Mom?

When our daughters look at our lives, what do they see?
Are you telling your daughter she must get an education and
make something of her life like you never had the chance
to? Or are you teaching your daughter to *love learning*?

If you give your daughter the gift of love for learning,
she will learn all her life. But give her pressure to earn top
grades and be the best, to get out there and achieve like you
never had the opportunity to do, chances are your daughter
will wind up in front of the TV set just like you, soaking in
the soap operas and hiding nasty sado-masochistic romance
books in cupboard drawers. She never learned that learning
is the most exciting gift of life. She may not be able to walk,
but if she loves to learn, she will never be crippled.

I know of some mothers who teach their daughters that
the most important values in life are found right in the
kitchen under the sink—where the cleaning supplies are
kept. But of all the happily married men I've ever talked
with or interviewed, none of them said they married a girl
for the way she could fold socks or scour a broiler. Preparation for marriage is not a matter of knowing how to do the
laundry. Men don't dream of marrying maids; they dream
of a friend, a partner, a lover. Isn't that how our daughters
should be dreaming and praying, too?

The daughter may question the value of this high calling
of cooking and cleaning when she sees her mother's dissat-
isfaction and frustration. Will she wind up like her mother—
married to a man who isn't fun or playful? who is often out
of town and enjoys it? who turns off the TV program she's
watching without even saying excuse me? who calls her

dumb and says things like, "Oh, you wouldn't understand," and "Here, let me do that"? What if she ends up like her mom, lying and sneaking around if she wants to do something or buy something he might not agree with? Will she always have to wait on somebody who never waits on her? Will she have to spend her life in the kitchen with the women gossiping, while the men gather in the other room discussing the real issues of life, such as politics, art, music, literature, even sports?

Teach your daughters to be persons, to be creative, confident, intelligent women of God, going forward, not backward. Teach your daughters not to minimize their personal strengths, to build their self-images based on the Word of God, to rejoice in their abilities and gifts, to refuse to be manipulated by guilt and to give without fear or restraint. These can be our gifts not only to our children, our families and community, but to the future of the world.

What are we teaching our daughters?

Who would have guessed that maturity is only a short break in adolescence?

—*Jules Feiffer*

ALL THIS AND STILL NOT HAPPY

CHAPTER SIX

There is yet another type mother—not a martyr, not even interested in being one. She is Casual Mom, the Woman Who Has It All and Is Pursuing More. She's modern, she's in the know, she's thin, she's educated, productive, and her relationship with her child begins and ends with a perfunctory "Good morning, dear."

The outstanding feature of this woman's home is the lack of closeness. The family members use personal pronouns like "darling," "dear," and "honey" in place of meaningful conversation. The husband comes home after a discouraging day and says, "I've had a terrible day. Everything went wrong." She says, "Oh, honey . . ." *Period*.

Moments of true sentiment are rare, yet it is quite common for these parents to refer to their offspring as "droopy drawers," "stinkweed," or "snotnose" in the most affectionate tones.

Casual Mom is incredibly concerned with outward appearances, good manners, good grades, good tennis, good looks, but only for good show. Liz Smith humorously speaks of this type mother whom she refers to as the WASP mother. She says she enjoys children most when they hit eighteen

and take % *American Express* as their permanent abode.
"The Jewish or Italian mother will have an attack, a migraine and a long talk with the Pinkerton Agency if her child expresses a desire to bop off to Europe."[1] But Casual Mom ". . . has a party and gives Johnny the Eurail pass that she has already bought him."

Some of Casual Mom's frequent parenting expressions are:

- "It's none of my business."
- "It's your life. You have to live it."
- "I refuse to interfere."
- "You're free to choose your own friends."
- "I don't care what you major in."
- "Why tell me?"
- "I'm sure he's a nice boy if his father is a Sears executive. Sears stands behind everything."[2]

And here are a few more from the Christian Casual Mom:

- "The Lord is the parent of my children. He'll show them what to do."
- "If the kids don't want to go to church, I don't believe in forcing them."
- "It's not my place to sit in judgment."
- "Kids nowadays are much smarter than they were when I was young. You just can't teach them anything."
- "Long-suffering? I don't understand the word. I believe in *non*-suffering."

Casual Mom is aloof, detached. She is not interested in helping her daughters find their identity because she is too concerned with her own. Her sons are treated as people who

---

[1]Liz Smith, *The Mother Book* (New York: Doubleday, 1978).
[2]Ibid.

go their own way and need little parental interference. To this, she gladly complies.

She treats her husband as another child and calls herself a "liberated woman." She does not understand the biblical principle of being joint heirs with her husband; she doesn't understand being partners in the kingdom of God as husband and wife, dedicated to each other's pursuit of fulfilling God's will, and parents of other human beings. These other human beings are left pretty much to their own devices with few restrictions, not because of a permissive philosophy in child-rearing but because of parental lack of interest.

But happiness and fulfillment that is sought from selfish motives is ill-balanced, disquieting and transitory. We are called to live in the joy of communion with Christ, to walk and teach our children the light of His love and the comfort of His presence. In this high calling there is the peace and protection of discipline and the call to excellence.

Examine the following list of ways we hinder the spiritual development of our daughters. It is written from a negative viewpoint to emphasize exactly what these traits and attitudes do to our daughters when they go unchecked. Can you see how *your* inner development has been impaired? Share this list with your daughters, your husband, your sons. Discuss as a family which points hit home.

Growth Stoppers:

1. Encourage your daughter to work hard to win the approval of other people at the expense of her own integrity.

2. Teach your daughter the tricks of acting phony and to act the way you think others expect her to act in order for her to gain acceptance.

3. Teach your daughter that she is acceptable to you only if she does, says and acts the way you say she should.

4. Be sure to do your daughter's homework for her because it's more important for her to get good grades than

it is to learn. After all, she's just going to get married anyhow.

5. Run to the medicine cabinet and the doctor every time your daughter has a pain or disorder. Teach her to believe that medicine is the only healer, that she needs help from outside herself and God every time she hurts. This will help her appreciate drugs and alcohol later on in life. "I *need* an aspirin" can then be replaced by, "I *need* a drink."

6. Don't teach your daughter to love and respect her own body. Teach her to be ashamed of her breasts, and to despise any imperfection on her skin or body. Be sure to tease her when she begins menstruation, and act pious with righteous indignation if she wears a skirt too short or a sweater too tight.

7. Don't teach your child by example how to dress tastefully and beautifully. Don't take her to have her colors done, and don't help her clothes shop. Don't discuss fashion with any knowledge on the subject except what *you* like.

8. Force your daughter to apologize even when she doesn't mean it. Demand a performance from her and tell her, "*I'm sorry* is not good enough, young lady." That way you provoke dishonest communication.

9. Force your daughter to lie to you because when she tells the truth you either don't listen, don't care or don't want to know about it. You can't stand bad news, so you'd rather not know the negative things that may be going on in your daughter's life.

10. Encourage tattling between your children and take your daughter's side every time your son(s) pick on her because she's the weaker sex. This teaches her to manipulate men and relish weakness.

11. Never admit it to your daughter when you're wrong or if you've made a mistake. That way your daughter will get the impression making mistakes is bad and it's terrible to be wrong.

12. Never say you're sorry so your daughter will learn

the joy and freedom repentance and forgiveness bring.

13. Never confess a sin out loud and never back down in an argument. This way your daughter will learn that only the weak give in and only the ignorant are sorry.

14. Be sure to teach your daughter to pretend life is terrific when it isn't, to act like she's happy when she's not, to appear successful when she's struggling and to appear perfect when she's far from it. This way she learns the nightmarish, frustrating life of the hypocrite.

15. Don't allow your daughter to express her opinions or to disagree with you. This way she learns her ideas are dumb.

16. If you listen to your daughter only to correct her and show her where she's wrong, she learns it's safer to be quiet and say nothing at all.

17. Don't take her seriously and make fun of her dreams.

18. Complain to your daughter about the problems in your life. Cry when things go wrong. Show her how to worry by your own exaggerated fears so she can learn women can't handle problems unemotionally.

19. Teach her by your own defeated attitudes that the way to handle problems is to let them wear you down and eventually destroy you.

20. Teach her winning is more important than participating.

21. Tell her it's not feminine to succeed.

Of course, these are not the values you want to teach your daughters, nor is this the vision of womanhood that you want her to receive from you!

These growth stoppers are the seeds of much mistrust, pain and defeat. *Growth builders*, however, always include the words, "I'm sorry, I'm growing, too" and "Will you forgive me and allow me to change?" Growth builders include genuine respect and kindness in spite of the mundane aspects of discipline and daily life.

God renews both mothers' and daughters' hearts in this amazing relationship when love says in our hearts, "My love for you is forever and I will help you grow. . . ." Love is gentle; love is kind. Love is not easily miffed and love *communicates*.

We're going to look at more of the special gifts we can pass along, but first we must look at the "dream" mother—the fantasy woman that many daughters dream of but no woman can live up to. Until we escape from this fantasy image, we are not free—neither mother nor daughter—to change and grow.

God wants whole people who live holy lives. Whether their title is Mother or something else, He is looking for wholeness.

—*Gladys Hunt*

FANTASY MOM

CHAPTER SEVEN

Daughters have fantasies of being perfectly loved and cherished by mothers whose only desire is to make the world a lovely place for daughters to live in. Fantasy Mom does not include nor does she bear any resemblance to an emotionally whole woman. She is a person who, at least in the mind of her daughters (and sons), should serve her family with joy and gladness and never ask for a thing in return. "Having you for a daughter is reward enough" should be a mother's delighted sigh as she advances more cash to her adored, precious girl, or irons her jeans, or prepares a sandwich for her.

No matter what, at any age, any time, Fantasy Moms should always be there for their children's needs. If the daughter doesn't thank her, obey her or respect her wishes, the mother must not complain or make unwarranted demands of her. Fantasy Mom is supposed to rejoice when her beloved gives her a card on Mother's Day and receive it as fuel for another year of undying service. When daughter needs her, Fantasy Mom is supposed to be prepared to drop everything to lend her listening ear, unlimited time and words of comfort (never advice) to the cause.

The primary job of Fantasy Mom, however, is not to just *serve*. Not just to be there, providing yummy food, making sure her daughter's clothes are presentable, and observing her from every possible medical and dental vantage point, ever delighted to finance her trips to the orthodontist, dermatologist, and department store. Fantasy Mom is much more. More than a loving, listening ear, a major lending institution, nurse, taxi, shrink, spiritual advisor, her highest calling is one only she can fulfill. No other human being on earth holds the power she does as the specifically ordained human being to *make the bad go away*.

The cry "Mommy!" at the first sign of trouble and opposition in life should ever be the signal for the loving, giving lifeguard to rush to the rescue. Never mind the age of the daughter. Daughters are never too old to cry for their Fantasy Moms.

Mothers should never die.

In preparing my research for this book, I talked with more than one hundred women about their roles as mothers and about their own mothers. I also talked to teenagers and grandmothers. Some of the stories I can share with you and some I cannot. There are universal truths we women share, no matter who we are or what our station in life. We need mothering, and though we may or may not have this need fulfilled in our youth, we are somewhat bound by it throughout our lives. We contrive a Fantasy Mom in hopes that there may actually be a person who will accept us, love us and serve us unconditionally. We cling to this unrealistic assumption, confusing it with need. Since it is never met, we either blame ourselves or the world around us. I am amazed at the incredible energy we spend being frustrated and angry that there really is nobody who will take care of us and make the bad go away, like the Fantasy Mom we believe in.

As one woman put it, "It was a shock to me to have to face my mother's lifestyle. I always wanted her to be my example, someone to emulate. I guess I wanted her to be so perfect, so strong, so good. Now I have to say, and painfully, that I really don't want to be like my mother. The reason is *she* never wanted to be like her."

An elementary-school teacher, age thirty-six, told me, "It was the biggest shock of my life when I realized my mother couldn't do everything." She went on to tell me she made the discovery when she was in high school, but was made to believe her feelings were the product of her teenaged rebellious spirit. Only now, after college and beginning a career of her own, has she allowed herself to believe her mother could never fulfill her Fantasy Mom expectations.

"I really believed, or at least I wanted to believe, that there was nothing on earth my mother couldn't do. Whatever need or conflict I faced in life, I always figured my mother could help me with it. Now it's still hard to face that she is a limited woman with limited intelligence, limited energy and limited resources."

Another woman in her thirties, who works as a free-lance journalist, made this confession: "It nearly killed me to face the fact that mother didn't have the abilities I thought she had. I mean, she is just plain inadequate in a number of areas. Sometimes she can be a real nuisance. I feel so guilty with this awareness. Like I don't have the right to even think such things. A person's mother is supposed to be beyond reproach, isn't she?"

When we face facts, press our nose up to the wiped-clean window of reality, we are shocked at the vision before us. We call our feelings "shattered illusions," but more correct is the condition called "growing up." Grown-up people can say, "You're not perfect and I love you."

Why, then, do daughters feel *guilty* when their mothers are not the women we dream they should be? Two reasons. One, the daughter's need for a perfect mother and, two, a mother's need to be perfect for her daughter. The daughter's heartcry is, "Take care of me, Mommy"; the mother's heartcry is, "Need me, my dearest daughter—don't ever stop needing me."

As much as I want my mother to make the bad go away and as much as I want to be a heroine to my own daughters, neither is realistic. I've worked hard at settling for friendship. Honest, open, loving, faithful friendship with the best friends I have in this world. And these friends of mine may sometimes disappoint me, hurt me, neglect me, insult me, use me, or make demands of me I can't meet. We don't diminish with such encroachments. We can handle the impositions as well as the blessings.

If I'm given the right to fail my loved ones at times, I am not saddled with the task of maintaining a fairy tale version of perfection. If I give them the right to fail me at times, they are free from the tyranny of guilt.

But making the decision to be friends takes work. Allow me to give you an example of what I have thought of (in the past) as reasonable, motherly strategy.

Wants:

We're talking fairness, equality, justice and friendship here. I used to explain to my daughters that we each have wants, each have needs, each have minds to think and we each have feelings. I sermonized, with impressive detail, on the fairness of it all. Then I spelled it out:

Me: I want you girls to know I respect you as human beings. You are not only my daughters, you are my friends. I choose to see you as young adults, not children who still require nurturing and caring for, as in the past.

In my mind the formula, however, looked like this:

I want — you want.
I need — you need.
I think — you think.
I have feelings — you have feelings.
I give — you give
I'm boss — you're not.

So much for equality. Some of our "democratic family forums" have sounded more like prison riots than exercises in mutual understanding and open communication. But what do you expect from a person who has been a mother as long as I have? My own mother told me every mother should receive a college education in motherhood. But by the time she graduates, the children are grown and moved out of state.

Independence is difficult when it goes against the mother's values. Techniques notwithstanding, when you're a conservative middle-class mother and the most radical thing you've ever done is to bleach your bangs, you're going to experience a conflict of feelings when your daughter doesn't share like values. When you suddenly find yourself facing a daughter with her purple hair scraping the walls and ceiling, her eye makeup done in early Salem witchery, her combat boots clashing with her mesh hose, you've got a values conflict. The way a teenager dresses is often a statement of how he or she sees himself. It tells the world what to expect of him or her. Further, it is group identification. The message "I'm one of this group or that group" is not as important as "I am one of," period. "I belong," "I'm a part of," "I'm accepted by" are crucial feelings for the teenager.

And Mom is excluded from this special place. No matter how accepted the teen is in his or her family, acceptance outside the family among peers is vitally important now.

The Christian parent often finds this period of parenting the most trying. Every undesirable act of independence by the child is viewed as rebellion and negative. There is constant conflict between parent and teen as the parent continues to assert authority and the teen continues to strive for independence.

One such case was a sad one I witnessed in my own office: A Christian woman called and, in a frantic voice, asked if I could please see her teenage daughter "as soon as possible." Things had gotten out of hand at home and it was an emergency situation.

The daughter came in—a beautiful girl; sweet, intelligent and a Christian. She wasn't exactly thrilled to be facing a counselor, but we became friends in a short time and she felt comfortable to be herself. She said, "My mother is always blasting me with the Bible." She told me she didn't think her mother was interested in anything except being right. She didn't feel loved, she felt smothered. She felt being loved by her mother was contingent upon doing exactly as she said.

"Why can't she accept me for me?" she asked. "Why do I have to be somebody she creates? If I do or say something that isn't what she would do or say, then I'm the wrong one. I'm rebellious. I'm not honoring my parent, I'm not submitting."

Look at the beliefs parents hold regarding their teenagers, and notice the reciprocal beliefs the teenager is likely to develop:

PARENT THINKS (Believes):	TEEN RESPONSE (and Believes):
She can't make right decisions.	I can't make right decisions.
She's stupid.	I'm stupid.
She can't take care of herself.	I can't take care of myself.
She won't make it.	I won't make it.
She's acceptable as long as she's "good"—conforms, goes to church, dresses right, doesn't disobey or act out.	I'm only worthwhile if I do as others want. Decisions I make for myself are not of value. Acceptance is hard work.

My underlying beliefs influence what my teenager and I think of ourselves. These beliefs can put a limit on what we can do, be and have in our lives. Having faith in my daughter's ability to make good decisions can act to enhance her ability to do so. My previous judgments about my daughter's decisions may have been too narrow. I didn't allow her to make mistakes. Her mistakes were some of her finest teachers.

The teenaged girl in my office didn't have that option because her mother allowed no room for mistakes. Drs. Robert and Jean Baynard, a husband-and-wife counseling team, suggest making "life piles," one for the parent and one for the teenager. The things the parent does not like about the teenager and his behavior goes into one or the other life pile. It either clearly affects only the teen, thus belonging in his or her life pile, or it has consequences in the parent's life and affects him and/or her directly. (Stealing money from a parent's wallet affects the parent; wearing outrageous makeup to school does not.)[1] We are advised to take the long view in our dealings with our teens, to drop the urge to push him or her to shape up in the specific situation and instead, ask ourselves, "What can I do in this situation that would contribute to my kid's being more responsible and able to make his or her own decisions?"[2]

The mother brought her teenaged daughter to me with the idea that I might be able to "straighten her out." I attempted to discuss with the mother her own rigid views that gave her a false sense of stability. She zipped right up. Closed tight. No, she would *not* consider herself in need of change or help. God was all she needed and the problem was her daughter. *She* was rebellious.

To this day the mother believes the daughter to be rebellious and "out of God's will." The daughter graduated from high school, went to the Bible college of her mother's choice, quit in the middle and eventually married a marvelous Christian man. They both attended Christian counseling

---

[1]Baynard and Baynard, *How to Deal With Your Acting-Up Teenager* (New York: M. Evans & Co., 1981).
[2]Ibid.

for a year, are active in their church and love the Lord with all their hearts. But the mother remains aloof and distant. Her daughter didn't marry the kind of guy she had in mind for her. In fact, in her mind, the daughter had fallen from grace as a teenage rebel and never ever found her way back to the straight and narrow "right" way. The only way, in this woman's mind, was *her* way.

Let's look at some positive godly alternatives to our "Parent Thinks and Believes" and "Teen Response" list. We can change the beliefs we have toward our teenagers and when we do, their responses will change, too.

PARENT THINKS:	TEEN RESPONSE:
My daughter is responsible for what she does.	I'm responsible for my own actions.
She can make decisions.	I can make good decisions.
She is a good kid.	I'm OK.
I trust the Lord to watch over her and help her succeed in all she does.	I trust the Lord to guide me.
I trust her as a Christian.	I am a Christian.
I can't make all of her decisions for her and I like it when she wants to talk about things she cares about.	Mom is interested in me and trusts me to make decisions that are right for me. I like talking to her because she listens.

I had to change the way I thought about my teenagers. I had to change my belief that I was the one who knew what was right for them and they had better do as I say or it's doomsville. My daughters were *not* helpless, naive youngsters, courting disaster and danger with every step. They were people, quite capable of making decisions and, besides, they had the right to make and learn from mistakes. Their lives were not in peril. God was on the throne, Jesus was still Lord and Savior and He could see us through these years just as He has seen us through every other phase of growth. I resolved to do everything I could to encourage my daughters to make their own decisions, even if they differed from mine. And I listened to their ideas without giving advice unless asked for. (Not always easy to do!)

People do not necessarily learn to be responsible simply by getting older. People learn to be responsible by being on their own and making decisions for which they take the consequences. I couldn't protect my children from the snares and darts of life by continuing to make their decisions for them. I couldn't save them from the armies of "dragons" out there just waiting to devour innocent, lovely children. Oh, how I wanted to walk before them, choose their clothes, their friends, their hours, their part-time jobs, their study habits, their hobbies, their sports activities, their studies, their life work, their boyfriends—*I* knew what was best. I, after all, had walked the highways and byways of life for a lot longer than they. Surely that qualified me as an expert, an authority.

Such thinking produced dialogue such as the following:

Me: You're not going to wear *that*, are you?
She: What's wrong with this?
Me: Are you kidding? You look like Meliva the Gypsy Lady.
She: Thanks a lot, Mom. That's a real nice thing to say.
Me: What did you expect? I actually thought for a minute that I was in a Stephen King movie.
She: If you don't like what I look like, turn your head.
Me: I just want to know one thing. Where can you go where they would accept you looking like that? That's what scares me.
She: Mom, you're really bugging me.
Me: *I'm* bugging *you*! I like *that*!

This scene can conclude in any number of ways. Doors

slam and raised voices dim in the roar of a broken muffler as some old wreck hauls "Meliva" and friends out of the driveway. Another scenario may be that said friends show up and Mom faints against the wall in the shock of realizing that her daughter is actually conservatively dressed in comparison to the state wild animal park in her living room.

But let's re-do the scene. Watch how I make an earnest effort to "let go" of overbearing parental control and begin to engage in trust.

She: How do I look, Mom?

The New Me: Oh, dear Lord . . .

She: Mom? You like it?

The New Me (gaining control!): Who would have guessed an old coat lining would go so well with crinoline?

She: Aren't these shoes great? I got them for twenty-five cents.

The New Me: How creative of you to wear lacy anklets with combat boots.

She: Do you really think I'm creative?

The New Me: Honey, you give a new meaning to the word.

She: You're probably the only person in the whole world who thinks I'm creative.

The New Me (really hearing her): You *are* creative, dear. And you're talented. I trust you to be talented and creative where it will benefit you most.

Anne Morrow Lindberg, poet and mother of six, once said, "I believe that what a woman resents is not so much giving herself in pieces as giving herself purposelessly."

Giving ourselves to understanding, caring and wise parenting of our children has to be one of the most purposeful activities we can engage in.

You may believe in the old, strong-arm method of straightening out your child. You may shriek and lock the child in her room when she displays in her mawkish, sometimes unpleasant ways, her desire for independence. But extremes always produce more extremes. Discipline includes understanding and mercy. We teach our children to be disciplined human beings by example and by rules that they must learn to obey and follow when they are young. The purpose of discipline is not to prove our own rightness, however, but to give our children the gift of its fruit: righteousness, holiness and peaceful hearts.

Today, my daughters no longer wear the same outrageous clothes they once did; they're full-time college students who enjoy learning. They work at jobs; they eat right; they're active in church and they love the Lord. Amazing. They're *responsible*.

If you look at your own life, you're not the same as you were yesterday, either. We change, grow, learn, grow some more. And thank the Lord, so do our daughters. Knowing these things allows us to release the "Fantasy Mom" ideal from our minds. If the kids can blow it, fail, make mistakes, so can Mom.

Fantasy Mom is the invention of children and parents alike. Mom herself may perpetrate the dream by the impossible image she insists she reflect. Someone once said, "My mom was up at 5:00 every morning no matter what day it was." Fantasy Mom wants us to believe she's perfect, selfless and without sin. She can do anything, would lay down her life for her loved ones. In Neil Simon's play *Come Blow Your Horn*, a mother pays a surprise visit to her son who is expecting a girlfriend to show up at his apartment any minute. "Listen, son," she says, " do I cook for myself? No, it's for *you* I cook. I myself haven't had anything but black coffee in ten years." Fantasy Mom doesn't eat. She lives for the family's stomach.

And, finally, Fantasy Mom thinks she should be and remain the most *beautiful* woman in the world. (This is the pressure we put on ourselves. Don't put the blame entirely on media hype and the Playboy philosophy.) Seventy-year-old grandmothers today are down at the gym at dawn ready to work out to keep their lithe figures. In every mother's bathroom cabinet there's a row of bottles and jars, enough to grease the state of Rhode Island for two years, all to help keep her young and to ward off the ravages of time. She perms, diets, exercises, sacrifices, shops sales so her loved ones can go on believing there's no one in all the world as beautiful as she.

With every passing year, she aims to fight time. Fantasy Mom must live out the aphorism: "You're not getting older; you're getting better."

Like Queen Nefertiti. This mother of six, married to Egypt's King Akhnaten, knew how to be a real live Fantasy Mom. Her little girl, Ankhesenpaaton (I was going to name my daughter after her, but chose the name Liza instead), married King Tutankhamen and the whole family became super-stars. All of Nefertiti's children were *daughters*. She had no sons. And she was proud of it. Today a painted limestone bust of Nefertiti is in a West Berlin museum. She's got the longest neck and most beautiful face in all of ancient art.

If they were to make a bust of you, what would it look like?

> *Many daughters have done nobly,*
> *But you excel them all.*
> *Charm is deceitful and beauty is vain,*
> *But a woman who fears the Lord, she shall be praised.*
> Proverbs 31:29–30

You can't be so unintelligent as not to realize that nowadays the only thing that counts is youth. And it's because we've discovered that, that our generation is so much ahead of every other. . . . In [Mommy's] time, when they were young, they just wanted to be older. . . .

—Somerset Maugham,
writing of the youth of the 1920's

LET'S HEAR FROM THE DAUGHTERS

CHAPTER EIGHT

Mommy's time may have been heralded by the drive for success and being older. But Mommy, today, is working hard to be younger. The fact that she has daughters to raise doesn't ease her plight. Her daughters lack her drive, her powers of self-denial and goal-targeting. They are just— well, just *young*.

At times, it's difficult for teenaged girls to understand why their mothers act the way they do and, especially, communicate the way they do. A teenaged girl may get the impression her mom is an archenemy, or just one big interference in her life. It's not too unusual for a teenaged daughter to wish her mother would just fall off the edge of the earth. A teen daughter may complain, "My mother is always bugging me, always nagging—she drives me crazy."

Mom may appear to be completely out of it and weird. Maybe she's too religious, too pious, too demanding, too uptight, or maybe she's just not *there* for her daughter. Maybe she's too busy doing her own thing. One sixteen-year-old girl told me her mother was more interested in men than in her children. She was out every night and brought a steady stream of different boyfriends home. The girl was expected to call them "uncle" so-and-so, and was now refusing to do as her mother wished. "None of these guys hang around for long anyhow; why should I be nice to them? I'm sick of *uncles*." Her mother accused her of trying to get in the way of her happiness.

Another teenager, eighteen, told me how her mother had raised four children alone and had given them each a legacy of love that would guide them all their lives. The last of the four daughters to leave home, she is following the footsteps of her older sisters and going to Bible college, then university to prepare for a ministry in missions. Her mother will be returning to the mission field also after what she humorously calls a twenty-two-year furlough.

"My father died in the Philippines when I was a baby, and Mom said her job then became to raise her children, not to be a missionary," the young girl explained. "Our home was always filled with missionaries and talk of missions. Now we'll all be going to the Philippines."

Do you have a legacy? Are you preparing one for your daughters?

Below are the words of seventeen females of all ages. What they have to say speaks for many hundreds of thousands of females. They tell us, in these short interviews or scenarios, of their roles as daughters. Sometimes their candor seems shocking. Each daughter claims to be a Christian, with either one or both parents professing to be Christians. Maybe you can identify with one or more. Read their frank, open words and then read the commentary at the end.

Which one is you?

Sue:

Being five years old isn't fun. People are big, scary. Mommy can be scary, too. She yells at me. I don't know why. I'm not naughty. I'm good. Mommy thinks I'm bad.

If you're like Sue, no, five years old isn't fun. Yelling,

overbearing adult behavior is frightening to a child. People who are violent to get their point across are unbearable at any age. Angry adults teach children that the world is a hostile place. They give the child little of what is trustworthy and secure. If you are like Sue, don't make excuses for your parents. Forgive them; allow the Lord to cleanse your heart of anger or fear toward them. Then be very aware of your own behavior, lest you, too, turn to yelling and overbearing behavior to get attention and/or express yourself in what you may perceive of as a hostile world. The way of God is always marked by gentleness. Do not accept hostile behavior in others.

Carrie:

I am seven. My birthday is in September. My mom gave me a Barbie doll for my birthday, and now I have nine, plus Barbie's house, pool and three cars. I asked Mom if I'll be as pretty as Barbie one day and she laughed at me. My mom always laughs at me. I hate it when she laughs at my missing teeth. I cried at the dinner table when she teased me, and she laughed harder. I'll never be pretty.

Carrie is too young to worry about her looks. If your mother made you ashamed of your appearance, if she humiliated you in any way, be sure you don't go on humiliating yourself with self-recriminations. Give yourself permission to be a beautiful and acceptable you.

Kelly:

I wish my mother would listen to me. She doesn't believe me. She thinks I'm lying when I'm not lying. My dad does things to me all the time. He hurts me. He tells me it's our secret. I can't tell anybody, because my mother said if I lie again, she'll send me away. Sometimes I think I'd rather be sent away than do what my dad makes me do. Is there a jail for five-year-olds?

Kelly, who was abused sexually, represents at least 600,000 children today. It doesn't matter what age you are now, if your father, brothers, uncles, neighbors, or any adult person, male or female, touched your private parts, you were being sexually abused. This is a crime punishable by law. Somebody violated your privacy and they were terribly wrong to do it. You can talk about it. You must talk about it. You must tell a teacher, counselor, pastor, or some other person who is prepared to professionally help you. The worst thing you can do for yourself is to bury your feelings and tell no one. The second worst thing you can do is to miserably dwell on your mother's reaction to what happened to you.

If your mother is like Kelly's mother, she needs help from outside sources to face the truth. You must concentrate on yourself and your safety, well-being and healing. Your life counts!

Jeannie:

My mother is so smart and good. I'm ten years old and I could never be as smart or as good as my mother. She never does anything wrong. She's perfect. I want to make her proud of me, but something always goes wrong. I get in trouble at school, but it's not my fault. Nobody believes me. My sister tries to get me in trouble and my mother listens to her. My sister is a brat.

Jeannie is never good enough for her mom. Her mother is "perfect"; how could Jeannie be good enough? If your mother is perfect, she may like it too much to change. You can try talking to her, asking her to listen to you, but chances are, she's going to stay perfect, at least in her own eyes. The thing you must guard against is losing your cool, because that will only make you look worse. Your sister may put you down or make trouble for you, but if you stay cool and calm, you will be amazed at your mother's receptiveness to you. She'll think it's a miracle.

Sondra:

I'm thirteen years old and my mother treats me like a little kid. It's awful. She doesn't trust me. She doesn't approve of anything about me, my clothes, my friends—nothing I do is good enough. My curfew is much earlier than all my friends. And what do you think my mother says when I come home on time like she wants? She just finds something else to complain about or yell at me for, like my hair or something. I can't wait until I'm old enough to move out on my own. Why can't she just accept me?

Poor Sondra. Her mother complains constantly. Nothing pleases her. This is typical mother behavior. Also part of the Perfect Mom syndrome. If you're like Sondra, you must sit down with your mother and ask her in your most affirmative voice if she would be willing to make an agreement with you to compliment you at least five times a day. Tell her nicely you would like her to say affirming, reinforcing words to you like: "You look so nice," and "You did real well," and "Thank you for coming home on time," and "I appreciate the nice things you do around the house," and "I love you and think you're a terrific daughter."

Then tell her the affirming, reinforcing words you will agree to say to her, too.

Kikki:

At day care, Miss Apple took my bottle. Why can't I have my bottle? Mommy gives me my bottle. Mommy loves me. Mommy is pretty. Mommy smells good. I'm going to tell Mommy to shoot Miss Apple. Then Miss Apple will be sorry, and Mommy will give me my bottle.

Kikki is not ready to be separated from her mommy. When you were four, were you ready to go to day care? Did you cry when your mommy left you? Are you still crying? Are you still looking for your bottle? Chances are, your baby-sitters loved you very much and genuinely cared about you. Just because you went to day care or a baby-sitter doesn't mean you were left without loving care. Most of the people who are in day-care work are there because they love children. It's time you began to be grateful for the loving care you've received in your life instead of complaining of what you erroneously think you didn't receive.

Cassandra:

I'm four years old. I hate it when I have to go places with my mom and her friends. Nobody ever talks to me. I have to just sit there. She tells me to hush, be quiet, don't do that, sit up, stop that—but there's nothing for me to do. Last time, her friend told mom she understood what she goes through, because her own daughter was a "holy terror" at one time, too. What's a holy terror? Is that what I am?"

Cassandra, you are not a holy terror. You are a good girl, a sweet girl. You are God's treasure. It's difficult to hold still and be quiet when you don't have anything to do and the grown-ups are all talking and ignoring you. Be sure to tell your mother what a good girl you are. And next time remember to take your dolls, books, paper and coloring crayons and other toys with you so you will have fun.

Peg:

I'm fifteen years old and my mother treats me like a little kid. She even has to go clothes shopping with me because she's afraid I'll buy something she doesn't like. Why can't she be a normal person like my friends' mothers?

They aren't even Christians, and I like being at their house better than at my house. Their mothers aren't so uptight and totally judgmental. They don't punish all the time. I'm really angry because when I was little I thought our Christian life was the only right life. Now I think of all the times I was hit and spanked—how may times my bottom was actually bruised and cut from the ruler—and I just boil. All those punishments, sitting in the corner, and now being grounded all the time.

I feel like my mother has robbed from me. Deceived me. Nothing good can be that cruel.

Peg needs to realize she will not change her mother. Only God can do that. If her mother is overly religious and un-approachable, Peg will only suffer more by trying to get her to see the errors of her ways. Peg's mom doesn't believe she's wrong. She really believes that, because she's the mom, she's *right*. She believes children require discipline, which is true, but her methods of discipline are harsh. She lacks warmth, humor and tenderness in child-rearing. Peg must forgive and turn to the Lord Jesus with all her heart for help. Obedience brings wonderful rewards, but rebellion only brings sorrow. Though the punishments are extreme and they surely seem cruel, Peg need not hurt herself more by getting mad at God or rejecting His help. She may one day punish herself the way her mother has punished her.

Donella:

I'm sixteen and my mother has worked at her job ever since I was six. So I've never come home from school to find her there waiting with cookies and milk, like some people say mothers are supposed to do. I don't know what the big deal is. My mom and I are real friends. She's the best person I know. I hope I can be like her one day. When we bake cookies, we bake them together.

Donella has a best friend: her mom. They do things together, go places together, play games, even exercise together. They share more than cookies; they share a rich and happy respect and love for one another.

Baby:

Mamma screams. Mamma hits. Mamma talks on the phone. Mamma won't lift me. Mamma! Mamma says I'm spoiled.

Please lift me, Mamma. No phone! No other people! Just me, Mamma! I want Mamma.

Baby faces rejection before she can talk. Perhaps most of us are babies. Renounce the urge to feel rejected, and while you're at it, renounce your fear of rejection. If you control those fears of rejection now, while you are young, you will have a skill for the rest of your life. View rejection as a healthy experience of life. We all need a little rejection to cause us to grow in compassion and beauty of soul. Stop thinking it's the end of the world. Babies can't see beyond the present moment. You can.

Cheryl:

I'm eight and a half. My mother is a witch. She turns my dad against me. I heard her tell him to tell me my pants are too tight. Then she tells me I'm fat. Now my dad doesn't like me and it's all her fault. I want my dad to like me. I wish he would take me somewhere, just me and him alone. But the witch won't let him. She always has to come along, and then they both ignore me. She even calls me fat in front of my friends.

Cheryl desperately wants the approval of her dad. She will get it as long as she reaches out to him herself instead of waiting for her mother to do it for her. She must ask her mother quietly and politely not to make mention of her body size to others because it hurts her feelings. Perhaps Cheryl's mother wants Cheryl's love and doesn't feel she has it, so she lashes out with barbs that hurt. In any case, Cheryl needs to spend time alone with *both* her mother and father.

Michelle:

Dear Jesus, please bless Mommy and Daddy, but most of all Mommy, because she's the sweetest, most precious-est Mommy in all the world, and she should be blessed tons and tons. Is that a good prayer, Mommy?

Michelle says just what Mommy wants to hear. Is it OK to say what Mommy might not want to hear? Should Michelle always work hard to earn Mommy's approval? What if Michelle makes a mistake and says the wrong thing? Will Mommy still love her?

Barbara:

I'm worried something might happen to my mom. She's always sick. I don't like to leave her. People tell me I'm a lot older than twelve, but that's how old I am, twelve, and I guess that's supposed to make me feel proud. I'm just worried and afraid for my mother. She's so weak and helpless. I can clean the house and go shopping for her. I don't want her to get hurt or to die. I pray every day for her and I tell God I'll give up anything at all—I'll do anything if He will just keep my mother from dying. I overheard some grown-ups who said she's not sick at all; she's just afraid of life. So I try to tell her not to be afraid, because I'll always take care of her. So far she hasn't heard me.

Barbara is too young to bear the responsibility of another person's life. She needs to be able to be a twelve-year-old and play and be carefree once in a while. The fearful burden that something terrible might happen to her mother if she's not there to protect her is too much for a child to carry on her shoulders. She will only grow to resent her mother for not allowing her daughter's love and hard work to heal her. Counseling would help both this mother and daughter to overcome their inordinate dependency needs.

Terri:

One day I'm going to find my real mother. I'm going to ask her why she gave me up. I don't think I could ever give up a little baby who needs her real mother. How can mothers do that? I think about her all the time. I wonder who she is, what she is doing, if she's pretty and if she ever thinks of me. . . . Do you think she remembers when it's my birthday? That's today. I'm thirteen.

It is especially difficult for Terri when her birthday comes around. She thinks of her natural birth mother and torments herself with questions of why her mother didn't want her. Terri must learn to appreciate her life with her adoptive parents and understand God has given her His best. She must not put high expectations upon that "one-day" meeting with her birth mother who may be a very ordinary person who had no means of raising a baby.

Rebecca:

I'm eighteen and in three weeks I'll be going away to college. I had mixed feelings when I received the scholarship, because it means I have to leave my mother. I don't know who'll protect her from my father with me gone. My father is an alcoholic, and he gets really ugly at times. He calls my mother filthy names and insults her horribly. My mother is a good person, quiet, shy, passive. She's too sweet. It infuriates me to see her treated so badly. But she refuses to leave him. I've begged her to leave him. I told her I'd work to support us and go to college later, but she won't hear of it. She says she can take care of herself, but I know without me at home there'll be no stopping his abuse. I totally hate that man.

Rebecca has to let her mother go and allow her to fend for herself. No child should ever be placed in such a position. Rebecca is at fault as well as her mother. Now that she's eighteen she must dedicate time to her education and her own future. Her mother will now be forced to take care of herself and stand up for herself. Though Rebecca doesn't believe her mother can help herself, maybe she is underestimating her mother. This is a family that would benefit from counseling. Rebecca may be happily surprised one day to see the Lord Jesus work a genuine healing and restoration in that household beginning with her mother! Love and faith are what melt and transform hearts, not fear and hatred.

Gwen:

My mother always taught me to accept a woman's lot in life. In other words, women are secondary citizens, unworthy, lowly servant-types. She taught me the way to get a man was to serve him. Well, my mother really screwed me up. I've been serving men for thirty years and it's gotten me nothing but older, dumber, poorer and less desirable to everyone. My mother taught me the way to keep a man was to serve him. I don't know why I thought it would work for me when it didn't work for her. Now that I'm worn out and tired after raising a family and taking care of a husband, he leaves me for another woman. Like my father did. Even my own kids don't respect me. Why should they? I don't respect my mother, either.

Gwen doesn't respect her mother, and no wonder. Look at her criteria. But surely her mother did something well in her life, had some good qualities and made some worthwhile contribution to this world. She couldn't have been so one-dimensional as to have been interested in only one thing— to be a slave to males. Surely she touched other lives in some way, surely she was a blessing to people at some time.

Gwen is angry at herself and, because she has followed in the footsteps of her mother's mistakes with men, she is angry at her mother, too. Her father dumped her mother, and now Gwen's husband has dumped her. And she had worked so hard to make his life happy. She served him dutifully and submissively like she was taught a good wife was supposed to; she had sacrificed, given, worked hard. And now her life lies in ruins. She feels too old and tired to start over. Besides, she thinks nobody would want her.

It will take Gwen time to reorganize and rebuild. It's important she allow herself time and important she have a support system to help her on the upward climb. Her church, prayer group, Bible study—all of these are crucial now. The worst thing Gwen could do is to retreat into her pain and isolate herself from Christian fellowship. Her Christian friends will affirm her, love her, encourage her, stand by her. Gwen's self-esteem is sub-zero now, and only God's love can do the deep penetrating work that is necessary to give her a new sense of worth and value.

Ruth:

My mother loved us kids and gave us the happiest, sweetest childhood. When I think of growing up, I think of one person: my mother. She was always there, always giving, always making things happy. Whenever we were sad she told us funny stories or played with us. She made things so special—even simple things like going to the park or having hot chocolate before going to bed were like events. Now I feel sad for those years. It's not a happy thing to be a grown-up in a world where things are uncertain and unhappy. I'm thirty-two years old, own my own business and I'm a success at it—but sometimes I wish I was a little girl and my mommy was here to make everything happy again.

Ruth is giving herself clear messages that she is avoiding or refusing to hear. She says she misses her childhood life of safety and security and she wishes she had her mommy. But in reality, Ruth is old enough to be her own mommy to herself now. The message she is giving to herself is that she needs to build her sense of security from the inside out. The Lord Jesus is her hero now. "The name of the Lord is a strong tower. The righteous runneth into it and are safe." The healthy way to miss and love her mother is to miss and love her for what she is *today*, not for what she was yesterday.

The people who tell us that mothers are perfect are usually mothers. Daughters may not agree. But every female person is a daughter, most of the time believing herself to be imperfect. What does this tell us? Are we silly, ignorant twits one day and then when our first baby is laid across our laps, we are suddenly transformed into creatures of wisdom and omnipotence, like our own moms were supposed to walk in daily?

Every one of us has a maternal image to reckon with, whether our own mothers have been good role models or not. And, as far off in the distance as it may seem, eventually most females become mothers. By natural birth or adoption, history shows us most female persons choose, voluntarily or involuntarily, to follow the maternal path. The question is, how hard are we able to work to emulate the merits of our own mother?

Mother as a comforter is certainly one crucial aspect of mothering most of us believe should be of the same importance as the very name "mom." In the next chapter we'll look at this comforter role of mother.

Take away love and our earth is a tomb.

—*Robert Browning*

MOTHER AS COMFORTER

CHAPTER NINE

When I was five we lived in an apartment in St. Paul, Minnesota. There was a scrubby patch of grass in the front, flagstone leading up to the building and trees that walled us in from the warmth and light of the sun. My little room was at the side of the hall across from the bathroom, and it had one window facing north and a closet. The window looked out at a fence, and in my closet I imagined a secret kingdom of queens and kings and princes and princesses behind my dresses and my shoes. I don't ever remember the sun shining in that room, but it was my room and that made it more magical and special than any other place in all the world. It was my happy little space where all my treasures were kept.

When I was five I became ill with pneumonia and the room became filled with sickness. Chicken pox, measles, pneumonia—all happened in that room. Pneumonia was the worst. My mother covered me with sheet tents and bathed me in steam. She wrapped me in towels and spooned hot broth into my mouth. She sat beside me and watched as the hot kettle puffed steam into my tent, just in case I moved and accidentally tipped it. She placed the radio beside me so I could hear music. I remember the sounds of my mother moving about in my little room. I remember my mother's touch, her smoothing my hair. I remember knowing that her hands did everything right. She fixed my tent. She made the steam so I would get well again and be able to breathe without coughing. She washed my cheeks with a cold cloth. I was not afraid. I didn't worry. (Those feelings I learned much later in life for far less serious reasons.) As a child of five with my mother hovering over me, I was unafraid. I didn't know she was fighting for the life of her daughter, determined to conquer the demons of pneumonia and death with her tools of home remedies, love and bone determination.

Nearly twenty years later I came down with pneumonia again. It was in New York City, and I lay in a hospital bed. I received antibiotics, there was an oxygen tent, electric steam and heating pads, but the loving hands and sounds of my mother moving in the room were not there.

My little girls and their daddy came each day and waited outside beneath my hospital window for a glimpse of me. And so every day I could look down and see the people who loved me, so tiny and far away in the color and energy of the outside world. Even if it was only a twenty-second glimpse, a weak grasping of my fingers against the windowpane, I saw them, my family.

My mother had no sophisticated equipment, no antibiotics to heal me when I was five, yet I became well. And years later in that hospital room, feverish and choking for air and life, my family waving and smiling at me, I remembered that Jesus told us love conquers all. I became well.

There have been other times in my life when I have been gasping and choking for breath, but not with physical illness. Perhaps the cares and stresses of life were crushing or my heart was broken, and I longed for the quiet, confident sounds of a loving mother in the room. She wasn't there.

These moments when nobody knows you're dying except you—nobody else is sitting up with you as you cough on your troubles in the night—these are the moments to reach out for the mother-love of Christ. We Christians don't have a problem seeing God as the Father figure, but we often forget that He is all in all. If mankind is created in His image, that includes women, and to view Him only as paternal is to limit Him. He is maternal as well.

> In the day when God created man, He made him in the likeness of God. He created them male and female, and He blessed them and named them Man in the day when they were created. (Gen. 5:1b-2)

I have learned to recognize the Lord's maternal loving-kindness as well as His paternal power and glory. He considers His daughters to be "as corner pillars fashioned as for a palace" (Ps. 144:12b), and when I am weak with hurts too great for me, I call upon my Holy Father-Mother God and Savior who sustains all who fall, and raises up all who are bowed down (Ps. 145:14); I reach out to Him who is gracious and merciful, slow to anger and great in lovingkindness; He is our Lord who is good to all, whose mercies are over all His works (Ps. 145:8-9).

I am a woman and I can never be a father to my children. A man cannot be a mother. We are uniquely male and female, and though we may perform tasks and functions of the opposite sex, we can never, nor should we try to be what we are not. The reason is, though we may have to carry responsibilities of both father and mother roles, only God is paternal-maternal. We, in His image, can find in ourselves the wisdom and guidance of His Spirit. We recognize Him in all His attributes. Our one desire in life is that He express himself in us without our limiting Him. Therefore, we can function without role confusion.

Though I am not tempted to turn from the Lord in overt sin, I can all too easily turn from peace and trust to enter the realms of worry, fear, sometimes even panic. I sin against innocence with my fears. It is a continuing experience to daily recognize His voice, His gentle, caring movements in all of life. I find it the most gratifying transaction to allow His heartbeat to be heard in my own.

What a humbling experience to allow the Lord to soothe us, comfort us, ease our fears and reassure us that all is in His wise and loving care. This calming of the raging soul is the Father's gentle, maternal will. I can hear Him at times, a smile in His voice, soft, smooth, calling me from across the waters, "Marie—Marie, come back . . ."

And I do.

Once we are young, then we're
    not anymore.
We hurry to pursue all our
    dreams.
But when we are old we're there
    for so long
That being young never happened
    it seems.

GROWING TOWARD INDEPENDENCE

CHAPTER TEN

My mother has always been my friend; I've believed that. When I was young she asked my opinion, and when I gave it she didn't correct me or tell me I was stupid. She listened to my ideas, she seemed to enjoy what I had to say, and what's more, she approved. I was a child with dreams. I was going to be something, do something wonderful with my life. I was so eager to grow up, to be on my own, to begin to make my dreams come true.

When I was seventeen, tottering on new high heels, I boarded the train at the Minneapolis depot with my girl-friend, Mary Jane, a young actress who was fresh from a summer of apprenticing at the Old Log Theater. We headed for New York City to pursue careers in the theater. I can still see my mother, father, sister, brother, aunts, uncles, my boyfriend, Darwin, and my best friend, LaRee, standing on the platform. They were waving, jumping up and down, some crying, waving. I think of that now and wonder how in the world I could have been so crazy as to leave them. Today, wild horses couldn't persuade me to leave so many people who loved me.

But I also know love sets us free.

To me, the world was not yet hostile. To me, the world was still a bright and beautiful place to chase rainbows, paint pictures, write poems, sing and dance. I figured I was ready for the Big Time; after all, I had studied ballet and musical comedy from the age of six or seven. I had performed in umpteen plays and musicals. I'd been on TV, my picture had been in the paper; I even won a few contests and scholarships as a young actress and dancer. Will Jones, the columnist for the Minneapolis *Star* and *Tribune*, wrote a special piece on me; I'd been interviewed on the radio and even had star billing in a touring children's theater group. I'd studied with Dr. Whiting and Dr. Ballet at the University of Minnesota while still in high school. I'd been in university productions. Oh, I was ready all right. It was a Judy Garland kind of world; the Big Apple was just waiting for me.

Mary Jane and I arrived starry-eyed at Grand Central Station, and I can still smell the filmy air of that gray morning. I wrote poems about it for years. It stuck in my throat deliciously, smoky and iridescent. We drank the milky coffee, bought the trade papers, rushed along with hoards of people who all knew where they were going. Mary Jane and I. She was even more the small-town girl than I, if that were possible. She was twenty-one, with bright-red hair and no makeup, wearing a pleated skirt and gray sweater set complete with saddle shoes, and straight out of prep school.

There are a number of choices parents make to help their children learn independence and self-reliance. Sometimes we rush our children and treat them as if they are merely smaller adults. I was a precocious child, I know that, and I rushed my parents. They may have wanted me to be a child a little longer, but I was eager, passionate to get on with my life. A sense of urgency began in me when I was very young, so long ago I can't ever remember being without it—a feeling that if I don't hurry and do whatever it is I must do right away, I'll be dead and it will never get done at all. Maybe it was Longfellow's poem about footprints on the sands of time, or something equally maudlin that drove me.

At fourteen I lied about my age and was hired at Bridge-man's Ice Cream Store in Dinky Town, Minneapolis, a block from University of Minnesota campus and my high school. I scooped ice cream, making triple treats and banana splits and turtle sundaes for three years, scooping away to pay for my ballet classes and classes at the university while attending high school and also during the summers when I was a full-time student at the university, studying acting and theater production.

I scooped peppermint bon bon and tutti-frutti and revel fudge until I graduated from high school and *TV Guide* hired me as proofreader. Now my parents could really see me function in the adult world. I wore dresses to work, caught the bus at 6 a.m., bent over galleys all day long, brought home a full-time paycheck; I was a high school graduate, a working girl, a child with a dream. I was out there in the literary world. I no longer scooped ice cream. My father called me Re Re Button Beezer until the day he died, but I wanted to be grown-up now. I was seventeen. I told them I was ready to move to New York to try for the Big Time. And they believed me.

I convinced my family that I was fully capable of suc-ceeding in a city like New York City with no help, no con-tacts, little money and very little professional skill. In spite of the seven-to-ten dance classes a week I'd taken in Min-neapolis and my considerable drive to achieve, I could hardly compete with the virtuosos in that city. I had to hurl myself into studying with the finest teachers in New York— voice, dance, acting, art, mime. I had to support myself as secretary, waitress, researcher, Santa's elf, junior-wear fash-ion model, children's dance teacher. I worked for a Broad-way producer for a while as a publicity assistant. I did voice-overs and character voices for radio and TV. If that's not eclectic enough, by the time I was married and gave up my dream of being show business's next Judy Garland, I had starred in over thirty summer stock musical productions, had appeared in plays and musicals off-Broadway (as well as standby *on* Broadway), three motion pictures, and toured in musicals and children's theater.

Dear Mom & Dad:

I love New York! It's beautiful and wonderful and so exciting. I can't believe I'm actually here! Mary Jane and I moved into our new apartment and already have a third roommate, another student at the American Theatre Wing. She's from Hyannis Port, Mass. The apartment has a fireplace! Tomorrow I have an audition. Today, I went to my first dance class at Carnegie Hall. Imagine! I miss you.

Love, Marie

P.S. Is it all right to call home collect?

36 West 71st. Street, NYC, NY

Dear Button Beezer:

The house isn't the same without you. We all miss you. LaRee called to see if we'd heard from you yet and Darwin called, too. Are you eating? What is your new roommate's name? Hope your audition went real well and you'll be telling us all about your new contract for a starring role on Broadway!

We love you,

Mom and Dad,

Corrine and Bill, too.

P.S. Yes you may call collect in case of an emergency.

As daughters, we learn what the word responsible means in a number of ways. First, by experience.

As children, we learn that if we disobey, we are responsible for the consequences; as pre-adolescents, we learn that we are responsible for our behaviors and attitudes about achieving or not achieving; as adolescents, we learn we cannot blame others for our faults or problems in life. And as adults, we learn not to depend on others for our sense of identity and self-worth.

Starting early, as babies in the arms of our mothers, we learn:

"Beautiful baby, gift from God. . . ."

"Mattie, for godsake, leave the child alone. . . ."

"Please, Grandma, give me my Johnny Panda Bear. . . ."

"Yes, dear, you have our blessing to pursue your dream. . . ."

"But why did daddy leave, Mamma? We're good Christians, aren't we. . . ?"

To live is to change, and to be perfect is to have changed often.

HOW CAN WE CHANGE?

CHAPTER ELEVEN

Unhappy people are the ones who are most afraid of change. The world is changing constantly. People change. Times change. I've heard women say, "But I've always ironed my husband's underwear. I'd feel guilty if I changed." Even though the woman works full time outside the home, she feels obliged to keep the same routine her mother did twenty years ago. Unsure of herself, confusing her work with *herself*, this woman goes on over-doing, over-working, over-extending and never experiencing a real sense of fulfillment and inner peace.

An eighteen-year-old daughter told me, "My mother expects me to keep on with my flute lessons and never ever give up. She still sees me as a little girl playing in the elementary school band. Why can't she see I've changed? "

A mother of two pre-teen daughters laments, "My daughters complain and make me feel so guilty because I go to school two nights a week. They're used to my being there for their every beck and call whenever they want me. Now they have to pitch in and help and actually do things for themselves. It's hard for them to accept this change."

"I hate change," says a grandmother with two daughters

and three granddaughters. "It used to be the kids stayed home until they were married; now they want to run off and live on their own before they're even dry behind the ears. And women? If you ask me, they didn't know a good thing when they had it. I was perfectly happy staying home and caring for my family while Henry went out and earned the living. I didn't have aspirations to be a bank president or an astronaut like today's women."

Then her sad after-note: "But when Henry died, I didn't know what to do. I didn't even know how to pay the bills. I had never thought about things like the pilot light for the hot water heater, or where the circuit breakers in the house are. Worst of all, I didn't know the first thing about getting a job. That's just what happens to a woman when she's left a widow. Henry told me I was a good wife. I don't think there is such a thing as a good widow."

To live is to change. Women face change whether we choose it or not. Anne Morrow Lindberg said, "A woman must come of age by herself. This is the essence of 'coming of age'—to learn how to stand alone. She must learn not to depend on another, nor to feel she must prove her strength by competing with another. In the past, she has swung between these two opposite poles of dependence and competition, of Victorianism and Feminism. Both extremes throw her off balance; neither is the center, the true center of being a whole woman. She must find her true center alone. She must become whole. . . ."[1]

Twenty years later, after the death of her husband, Charles Lindberg, Anne Morrow Lindberg examined her own words and faced again what she called "woman's recurring lesson." She said, "The lesson seems to need relearning about every twenty years in a woman's life."[2] This wholeness, this finding the true center of our being is dis-

[1]Anne Morrow Lindberg, *Gift From the Sea* (New York: Random House, 1955, Vintage Books Edition, 1978).
[2]Ibid.

covered in surrender to Christ.

Christ is the author of change, of an ever-rotating, evolving, moving universe. No single moment or motion is the same as another. "Behold all things have become new" is the heartbeat of each breath. We are products of and initiators of change. The core of our personal worlds as Christian women is locked tightly into the majesty of God. Though all He does and all He creates changes and moves and evolves, *He* never changes. He is the same yesterday, today and forever. His love, His faithfulness, mercy, concern and ability to lift us above the limitations of our own earthly flesh are always the same. Because He does not change, we can fling our souls into His and learn the skills of wisdom we need to live dynamic, meaningful lives in a world of uncertainties and changes.

When I was a teenager I wrote a song called *Nothing Lasts Forever* and some of the rather depressing lyrics went:

> Nothing lasts forever,
> Nothing's here to stay.
> What I loved best yesterday
> Now has gone away. . . .

I remember sniffing away the tears as I wrote the song, and even when I play it on the piano now, I get a sour little lump in my throat. But I must remind myself that nothing is *supposed* to stay. This is a world of change! Only Jesus and His loves lasts forever. We simply must come to peace with change.

People change. Times change. Things change. *Streets* change. I lived in a loft in New York City on 26th Street. Every day I walked on the same street, saw the same stores, the same buildings, the same traffic lights, the same doors and windows and sidewalks and curbs. And one day I walked outside and an entire building on my block was gone. *Gone*. It was there one day and the next day the whole thing was razed to the ground. Pebbles, bits of concrete, broken glass and wood splinters were all there was left to an entire building! No more windows, floors, desks, telephones, elevators—nothing. There was a great intrusion of sky where a building once stood.

Things change. We can give our children a sense of security that doesn't depend on sameness. Only love, God's love, remains the same. We're safe in Him, not in sameness. We're safe in Him, not in buildings. We're safe in Him.

In *Him* we move and live and have our being.

I know an older couple, Clara and Phil, who have lived in the same house for fifty-two years. They stay home for holidays and have never seen another city's Christmas lights. They haven't moved since they were married fifty-two years ago, so they have never unpacked boxes of dishes or tried to figure out where the sofa should go in a different living room. They've never seen another view from the window in the bedroom, never had to make friends in a whole new neighborhood—fifty-two years in the same house on the same block in the same town. They don't like to think about change.

Clara and Phil rarely leave the house. The car stays in the garage; they don't go for drives just for the fun of it. They haven't spent a night in a hotel in twenty-six years. They've never tried mahi-mahi, sushi or kiwi. They've never had pizza for breakfast, flown in an airplane, or snorkeled. They stay home where it's safe and the same. The food, the weather, the view—all the same. No changes.

It makes Clara and Phil angry that their daughter moved out of town and made her roots somewhere else. They don't go visit her, and they are deeply upset and hurt when she doesn't visit them, especially on special occasions like birthdays and anniversaries. Their daughter brought change, and Clara and Phil's resentment for this runs deep. After *all* they did for her.

There was a tree on the lawn in the front of Clara and Phil's house, a big elm tree. Every autumn, Clara and Phil knew just where the leaves should fall and how many of them would cover the lawn. One day, the city came by with their big tree-chopping truck and tied a red ribbon around the tree. Dutch Elm Disease, they said, and chopped down the tree.

Now there are no more autumn leaves on the lawn. It was an unbearable change. Clara and Phil stayed depressed for weeks. Not because they loved the tree but because they couldn't stand change. It was as if, for them, they lost control. The world they so valiantly fought to keep the same had finally overtaken them, and they lost to a gaping, mocking hole of sky, now invading the space where their trusty, familiar tree once stood.

We say words like, "You never know what to expect," as if it were a pronouncement of doom. "There's trouble behind every bush" and "get ready for the unexpected" are scary sentences. In order to give to our children the joy of life that we receive only through the Lord Jesus, we must give them a joy in change.

We can give our daughters a change of heart. A change of attitude. A change of communication. For example, if you're having a problem communicating with your teenager, you might resort to assaulting her with unpleasant attention-getters. Look at the following dialogue and see how, by changing tactics, you can open your daughter's heart to you and actually have a meaningful exchange:

Not So Terrific:		**Better:**	
Mom:	We never talk.	*Mom:*	What kind of day has it been for you?
Daughter:	Why should we? You just correct me or start a fight.	*Daughter:*	OK I guess, except I lost my glasses.
Mom:	I start a fight? I like *that*.	*Mom:*	I'm glad you had a good day. And I hope you find your glasses. You're good at finding things.
Daughter:	There you go again.		
Mom:	It's useless—impossible to talk to you!		

Daughter: I'm going to my room.

Mom: See? We never talk!

Daughter: I'm glad you have confidence in me.

Mom: I sure do. Now tell me about the rest of your day that went OK.

Not So Terrific:

Daughter: I never get to buy anything new. You don't care.

Mom: I just bought you new clothes!

Daughter: That was months ago!

Mom: Do I look like I'm made of money? You're so selfish. You don't care.

Better:

Daughter: I'd like to talk to you about earning some money for some new clothes. Is this a good time to talk? I'd like to help at home.

Mom: I'd like that too.

Try recreating your own dialogue with your daughter to match the above example. By reinforcing and giving your daughter a feeling of acceptance, you will open the channels of closeness.

Change is not easy. Change of attitude and change of place can be a difficult adjustment. In my book *Love and Be Loved*,[3] I write about my move to California from Minnesota in 1979 with my little girls who were then seven and eight. Change of place was a sudden jolt, an unexpected shunt into the unknown. I felt like Moses leaving Egypt for the Promised Land. It could have been a frightening experience, but instead we made it our true pioneering venture.

No one waited for us in California or really knew or cared if we were there or not. We created our own welcome. I had to present every day to my daughters as a miracle, a wonder. I had to teach them that an adventure waited around every

---

[3]Marie Chapian, *Love and Be Loved* (New Jersey: Fleming H. Revell, 1983).

corner for us. And it was extraordinary as we awakened each day expecting to be ambushed by joy.

We played on the beaches of gray sticky sand, rolled in salt-water waves; we climbed scrubby mountainsides and took pictures of the sunsets. We went to churches where the people sang songs we didn't know, we made new friends, found God in the desert and in the hills, in a condominium complex in La Jolla and on seamy Revolucion Avenue in dusty, crowded Tiajuana. We drove to Hollywood and put our hands in the handprints of movie stars. I screamed insanely on the Matterhorn ride at Disneyland. We discovered new insects and birds and plants and we ate mahi-mahi, sushi and kiwi.

Liza skied down our hill of ice plant. We wrote poems about sandpipers and sea gulls, drew pictures of palm trees and houses on stilts, gathered stones and shells, pasted dried flowers on pages of our scrapbooks, and took up cross-country running on the beaches and the hills. We met our new life in a strange place headlong.

Change should be exciting, venturesome. Try sleeping in a hammock or outside under the stars in a sleeping bag just for the fun of it. Ride a horse, buy a hat, spend a day in the woods, call your high school best friend, eat dinner in another town, learn Hebrew, discover something new every day.

The day we moved into our new condominium in California, I went out to the patio and it truly was a new world to me. It was so new, so *tropical*. New air, new breezes, new smells, new growing things. I looked down as I stood there in this enchanted place and I saw inching through the grass the most amazing creature. It was a garden snail, the first one I had ever seen. Intrigued, I called my daughters, "Liza! Christa! Come quickly! Come see what I found!"

We crouched on our hands and knees and marveled at this brownshelled phenomenon that we thought had come all the way up from the sea to visit us. We were extremely reverent and quite pleased with ourselves for our discovery.

When I tell this story to Californians, they howl with scorn. It didn't take us too many days before we learned that the garden snail is a horrible pest and people buy poison by the bucket to get rid of the miserable things. They ravage plants and flowers, leaving dime-sized holes in leaves. They ruin lawns and eat anything that grows. But that first meeting with one was wondrous for us.

To live is to change.

T. S. Eliot wrote in *The Love Song of J. Alfred Prufrock*,

To wonder, "Do I dare?" and "Do I dare?" . . .
Do I dare
Disturb the universe?

As mothers and daughters we can answer, YES! *We will disturb the universe!* As daughters of the Dream Maker, we can turn good into better, we can make something ugly into something beautiful and we can step on and destroy that which is an enemy of truth and beauty.

*Too often we give children
answers to remember rather than
problems to solve.*

—Roger Lewin

WHO IS THE REAL RUNAWAY?

CHAPTER TWELVE

Sometimes a refusal to change means deep mistrust and anger toward a world viewed as vast and painfully unpredictable. Elaine is one such person. Her story is important to share in this book because she embodies a cross section of the mother-types we have covered. Let me describe her to you:

To begin with, Elaine's home was always what some people would consider a model of the "normal" home. Two parents, three children, four bedrooms, two cars, yearly vacations to the lake; active church members. Elaine never worked outside the home and proudly told the world, "I'm a *full-time* homemaker." She wore this title as a sort of banner, her heroic helmet; her home was her monument of achievement and her badge of supremacy above other women.

Elaine always looked askance at those females in the church who "worked at jobs" outside the domain of their kitchens, bathrooms and family rooms, and wondered if it wasn't greed that motivated them. "Why do these families think they need so many 'things'?" she asked.

Everything was perfect in Elaine's world. She proudly

displayed her peach cobbler and her children's orthodontia. Her husband dutifully wore the clothes she chose for him, he did nothing rash like grow a mustache or drive his pickup truck to a wedding or a good restaurant.

Elaine was so proud of herself and so sure of her rightness that she was even dogmatic about it whenever she taught the women's Bible study at church. She was a manager of things and people.

Elaine had a daughter and this daughter played the piano, having studied with Miss Turbtwid, the church organist, for seven years. And this daughter was also an honors student at the Christian school she attended, *and* this daughter also won the Bible Olympics two years in a row. Sweet, obedient, well mannered, good teeth, this daughter was Elaine's crowning achievement.

But then this daughter, Bobbie, turned sixteen.

On a drizzly morning in October, Perfect Daughter with straight teeth, permed hair and neat socks ran away from home. Elaine was outraged at first, pacing the floor of her living room (done all in browns and beiges so as to remain neutral and not show dust or dirt so easily). She was furious. She ranted at her two sons, Brian and David, who were twelve and eleven at the time.

Elaine was fit to be tied. She even spilled herb tea on her Liz Clayborn slacks. "How could Bobbie do this to me?" she screamed. *"How could she do this to me? How uncaring and hurtful of her! Why?"*

Her husband, Bill, came home to find Elaine howling at the boys to do their homework, to shut off that TV and learn some responsibility in life.

Elaine let Bill have it before he got as far as the hall closet. "Where did I miss it?" she rankled. "What did I ever do to her? Haven't I tried to give her everything in the world? Why would she do this to me? I have always been there for her—I gave up my education to stay home and be a mother to my kids."

At first Bill didn't even know whom she was talking about. Then he figured it out. "But what happened? Did she elope?"

"*Your* daughter has run away," sobbed Elaine. "What will everyone say? Oh, she must really hate me."

Elaine didn't tell her friends that Bobbie had run away. She couldn't. She couldn't face the humiliation. She didn't call the police. Bill, against his better judgment, let Elaine handle the matter.

Life went on as usual. Elaine led the Bible study as usual, sat in church as usual, made her peach cobbler, folded the laundry—as usual. But she yelled, she screamed, she argued, she snapped at Bill every time he made a move she disapproved of. Finally, one night after she raved at him for not taking the garbage out when it was a man's job, after all, he quietly said, "I'll be leaving for a while."

And he did. Elaine was horrified. When he called home the next day to talk to the boys, she sobbed into the telephone, "Are you divorcing me? Do you blame me because your daughter left home? Haven't I been a good wife to you? Is this the thanks I get after eighteen years of marriage and hard work?"

Quietly, he said, "You make our lives a living hell. You've tried to make us all believe you're perfect, Elaine. I have felt guilty for years for not being able to meet your standards. I don't blame Bobbie for running away. She's staying at my brother's. We can't go on as we have. Things have got to change."

Change? What does that mean? To lose control? Elaine dove into a blur of activities and confused emotions. She scurried from prayer group to prayer group asking for prayer and seeking sympathy for the abandonment and "fallen" conditions of her husband and daughter. She wrote letters to famous preachers and evangelists asking for prayers for her backslidden family. She told people her daughter was on drugs and her husband was leading a wild life running around with other women. She hired a lawyer.

The truth of the matter was that her husband was going for Christian counseling and attending nightly Bible classes to draw closer to the Lord. And Bobbie was attending a new church, and involved in a high school outreach program. Both were staying with his brother and wife about fifty miles away. The boys eventually joined them, too.

Bill knew at the time he left he wasn't spiritually able to handle the hurt and discouragement he felt. He knew leaving wasn't the answer and he firmly believed divorce wouldn't solve a thing. So he pleaded with Elaine to join him in counseling so they could put the family back together again God's way. Elaine became so enraged she nearly passed out. Her doctor prescribed Valium. She began drinking wine in secret at home alone.

The nerve of that man, the nerve! He was the one who broke up the home. He was the one who condoned Bobbie's behavior. He was the one who walked out, taking with him every visage of pride she had ever hoped to have. He was the one—he, he, he.

This is a sad story because of the inevitability of its self-destruction. Especially pathetic are the role models of these parents. Look at Elaine: What did she teach her daughter about being a woman? What did she show her is wonderful, noble, strong or heroic about being a woman? What did she show her children about the character of the Lord Jesus? Did she have wisdom and beauty reflecting the Lord himself? Sometimes we're so busy teaching our children how wonderful *we* are that we forget we're supposed to be reflecting the personality of the Lord.

One day, in desperation, Elaine picked up the telephone and called my office. "Help me," she cried into my ear. "Please help me before I go mad."

Here's what she told me in our first session together. "Aren't there any rewards when you do everything right and you work hard to be the best and do a good job? I thought

I was a good mother. I sacrificed so much. I drove my daughter everywhere, I washed her clothes, cooked her meals, cleaned and took care of her every little need—look at the thanks I get. A note: *Goodbye. Don't try to find me. Bobbie.* "How can I ever forgive her? I *hate* her for what she did to me. And whom could I talk to? Not a soul on the face of this earth. Dr. Chapian, you are the only person I feel safe to talk to. My husband is a complete——. After eighteen years of marriage he walks out."

I wanted to hear more about Bobbie.

"A spoiled little——. It just makes my blood boil. All those piano lessons down the drain. I have never been more hurt in all my life. This may not sound very Christian, but I really hate her. I love her but I hate her. Those are my feelings exactly."

Elaine, up until now, had been unsuccessful in her attempts to rule her family and her little world with her demands and ideas of perfectionism. She could not forgive them for disrupting her intense efforts to rule perfectly. To be perfect.

Her anger was directed at them, not at an imperfect world or herself, but at those victims or "objects," as she treated them, who would not acquiesce to her wishes.

Elaine saw herself as a martyr. And martyrdom is the most essential of all the tools of guilt manipulation. Painful and powerful feelings of guilt are established by the martyr. When Elaine served a roast and took the burned piece, she always let her children know they got the better piece. She always made sure her children and her husband knew of her sacrifices for their well-being. She reminded them of what she went without for their sakes, how she never finished college so she could be home with the family, how she lived for her family. If she was not feeling well, she always did something special for them and told them about it. If these circumstances weren't present, she invented them.

And the rewards weren't there. They didn't worship her.

They didn't do exactly as she wanted them to. They still left their socks in the middle of the floor, still strewed dirty dishes and papers around the house with careless abandon. They still required nagging to mow the lawn, take out the garbage or wash the car.

In a session with Bobbie, she told me she ran away because she felt smothered, controlled and couldn't take living with her mother's manipulative and angry behavior. "I'm just never good enough for her, no matter what I do. I am never perfect *enough*. If I play a piano piece perfectly she says my skirt is too short or my shoulders are slouched. If I get an *A* on a test, she asks me how I'm doing on a paper I'm supposed to turn in. If I clean my room, she asks why I can't learn to hang up towels in the bathroom and why I'm such a slob. "I'm a disciplined person, at least I've tried to be, and she never gives me any credit. 'Why are you late?' she'll ask, but she won't say how nice I look and notice how long it took me to get my hair looking right. She hates everything I do, so why try to please her? I wore braces for three years and she still insists I wear my retainer twenty-four hours a day. Even the dentist said I only need it at night. But to her, it's like finishing your bath, and then taking a shower just to be sure you get all the germs.

"For a long time I worried about becoming a wimp like my father. He always seemed like he could care less. She just ruled him like he was a real worm, a nothing. He let my mother take care of the house, us kids, but just let one of us do something wrong, and he'd be right there to yell like she does. The day I left I swore to myself it was the last time I'd hear my mother screaming at me and telling me what I did *wrong*. And I was tired of my dad, who seemed like he could just turn off and not feel anything. Maybe that's how he wanted to live, but not me.

"Nothing is ever right enough for my mother. She just *can't* be happy or satisfied—ever. She should have had a perfect daughter who'd do everything right—I'm just not good enough for her."

Bobbie wanted a relationship with her mother but didn't know how to make it happen. The demands were too great to meet and she felt she always fell short of earning her mother's approval. Since approval usually means love, Bobbie did not feel loved.

"So I ran away. If you can call moving in with Aunt Nell and Uncle Ron running away. But I did it. I thought then she'd be sorry and see how much she really cared. She always told me Jesus loved me, but I wondered why when I was such a totally bad person. By the time I left I felt so really rotten about myself, about school, home, the works, I thought maybe I should just commit suicide.

"Then my father came looking for me. He said, 'You want to know how much I love you? I love you so much I'm willing to change and be a real dad.' We both cried so much. I could hardly believe it. I never thought he even cared about me at all; my mother always stood between us. Always had some chore to do if we were sitting around talking. Or she'd yell at him and tell him he never helped with us kids. So I thought he was a real loser, too."

Bill is a tall, thin man with gaunt features, long, slim hands and slow, deliberate movements. He speaks in smooth tones, barely showing teeth as he holds his mouth practically still with each word. His eyes are almost colorless, but there is a sparkle to them and as the conversation ensues, he occasionally allows himself to become animated, as if testing the listener for approval. His quiet passivity could be mistaken for control or even intelligence.

"I wasn't willing to lose my children. I could see what was happening to them. When Bobbie left, I knew it was only a matter of time before the boys would go their own way, too. It was like I didn't mind destroying my life, but I couldn't see destroying theirs. And I knew if I didn't do something, it would be too late. It was like I was addicted to pain. Like I had to have it or I didn't feel I was working toward being something. What that *something* was I didn't know.

"When I was young, my mother never gave me her approval, never hugged me, kissed me or told me I was a good boy. Through my therapy I think I realized being married to Elaine is like trying to earn approval from my own mother. Neither of them can give it. So I always have felt pretty worthless. Especially as a man. Inadequate. Elaine just reinforces that belief.

"I thought things would change when we became Christians. I mean, I didn't know *what* would change, but I thought maybe I'd feel happier. Maybe I'd feel more content. But I can't say that ever really happened. I'm a Christian and I love the Lord, but it didn't seem like He was hard enough on me. I was more attracted to the legalistic, hardnosed kind of Christianity where you're always put down because of sin. If I could, I'd get saved every week. I'd feel bad about myself, confess, repent and try to earn some kind of approval from God.

"I'm telling you, when I heard messages about God's *love*, I thought it was easy-believism. I didn't like it. It sounded phony and cheap to me. I saw God as hard, demanding and impossible to please. I used scripture verses like, *'Our righteousness is as filthy rags,'* and *'All have sinned and fall short of the glory of God.'* I can see now, I never in my life felt acceptable—to *anyone*.

"Then Bobbie ran away from home. It was like watching myself. She couldn't get her mother's approval, but she wasn't willing to hang around for the rest of her life working for it. I actually felt a little proud of her for making such a brave move. Isn't that terrible? Proud of your child for running away? I guess because she did what I wished I had the guts to do. It was an immature, wrong choice. But a little later I got the courage up to follow her. And then I went back and got the boys, too. We're all at my brother's now trying to sort out our lives.

"I never know what Elaine's feelings are. She doesn't want to talk to me, try to work things out or get some counseling. Sometimes I think that to Elaine we're just objects. Things. Game pieces to move about on a big board. Trouble is, it's a game of solitaire and she can be the only winner. I hoped when we left she'd really look at herself, join us in family counseling, try to change. We aren't giving up hope, but I don't really know if she loves me. Or if she ever has."

When I saw Elaine the second time, she was wearing a neck brace and taking pain medication for a spinal disorder. She bristled with anger as she spoke, her hands knotted in her lap, her mouth twisting and contorting with each word. "Nobody appreciates you when you give your whole life for them. Here I am, forty-two years old, thrown away like an old shoe. Even my kids have turned against me."

Elaine stormed against Bill and the family. She didn't want me to speak in our meetings and when I did she didn't listen. She was as obsessed with the idea that Bill, Bobbie and the boys were monstrous, hateful people who were against her as she had been obsessed with how wonderful they were when she was the model homemaker. But they were wonderful then because they were *hers*, not because of themselves.

She now told friends, "That man will crawl on his knees before he ever enters my house again."

But Bill didn't crawl. Neither did Bobbie nor the boys. People who love each other don't ask each other to crawl and ingratiate themselves. People are to be treasured, not manipulated and crushed. People who love each other don't demand control and power over the other.

Elaine had a lot to learn, but she refused to admit she was in any way responsible for the problems of her family. Instead, she disowned them. She wrote venomous letters to Bill's brother and sister-in-law for taking them in. She refused to see people as *people*, not objects. Her drinking increased, her health worsened. The saddest moment I witnessed was when Bobbie went to see her mother in the hospital.

I accompanied her and stood by the door as she inched her way toward the bed, where her mother lay staring at a blank television set.

"Mamma . . ."

The older woman's eyes darted to her daughter's face. Her face tightened and she said, barely moving her lips, "I don't have a daughter."

"Mamma, I came to see you because I want us to be friends." Bobbie's face was flushed, her eyes tender and hopeful. "Mamma, don't push me away any longer, please . . ."

"You think it's just that easy, don't you? You think you can march in here and say let's be friends, just like that, after what you've done to me, don't you? Well, don't ask me to do a jig, because I can't get up. I'm stuck with tubes everywhere."

"Mamma, I just want us to be friends, to be close like we never have had a chance to be."

Elaine was going to use every ounce of guilt manipulation she could muster up, but Bobbie wasn't buying it. When Elaine began to cough and sputter, Bobbie calmly handed her a tissue.

"In spite of everything, Mother," she said affectionately, "I do love you."

Elaine glowered.

"I've always wanted your approval. I've always wanted to feel like you *accept* me. I don't want to feel guilty anymore, Mother. I don't want to wish I had never been born. I want us to be friends, to love each other."

Elaine stared ahead, as though she couldn't hear. "Go away," she said flatly.

"Please. . . ? Mamma?"

The expression on Elaine's face hardened. "I have no daughter," she said.

This was the most supreme punishment she could come up with. The ultimate. She had her magnificent revenge.

But she didn't stop there. With an air of brilliant suffering and glory, she topped the rejection with these stabbing words, "Look what you've done to me." I shifted my weight and held my breath for the next obvious statement, and sure enough, she rose up on an elbow, fell back limply on the pillow, eyed her daughter square in the face and croaked, "When they lay me in the grave, Missy, you can just take all the credit."

If it weren't so tragic, I would have applauded.

Bobbie left and I stayed with Elaine the rest of the afternoon. I had her captive now, so I was going to take advantage of the situation.

I read to her, sang to her, told her funny stories and just sat there. I sat there when she snoozed; I sat there when she ate; I sat there when she received her injections, and when she used the bathroom. I simply refused to leave. Then she said to me in her special and unique nasty way, "Does it make you feel like you're helping me by hanging around all day?"

I told her I, too, was a mother, and that I, too, had a daughter who once ran away from home. I told her that very daughter who tore the heart out of my body was now one of my dearest and best friends on earth.

"Big deal," said Elaine.

"You have a daughter who has come back to you," I said. "She realizes she loves you and that with a little work on both your parts, you could be close."

She looked at me with the most pathetic look and whispered hotly, "You don't seem to understand *Doctor* Marie. *I can't forgive*."

I understood only too well. "But don't you deserve some love in your life, Elaine? Don't you deserve some happiness?"

She was agitated. "Love? Happiness? What's that?"

"It's letting go of your drive to control, Elaine. It's allowing your loved ones to make mistakes. It's allowing yourself to be loved and vulnerable. It's dropping your perfectionist ideals and opening yourself to a non-competitive, non-striving way of being and thinking."

"Big deal," Elaine retorted.

I wish I could tell you this story ended happily and that Elaine opened her heart to change, to growth and to the mercy and love of God. I wish I could tell you she discovered the lovingkindness of the Lord Jesus and that she learned the exquisite joy of forgiveness and renewal. I wish I could tell you the Holy Spirit restored that home, but to this day Elaine is somewhere out there on the streets, drinking, taking her Valium, running and angry. A few times a year she winds up in a hospital somewhere for broken bones or pneumonia and once for a blood clot in her leg, but she refuses to see her family. The divorce was final three years ago. Bobbie is married and the boys are both in college. Bill has not remarried and spends anywhere from ten to sixteen hours a day working and building a new company he formed and owns. He has not completely conquered the conflict between his need for social approval and his fear of rejection. Socially, his life is stilted and hurting, but his work takes up so much of his energy that he has little time to suffer with loneliness. The joy of his life is his daughter, Bobbie, and his two sons who love him dearly. You might even say he has a good life. That is, if you didn't know the full story, and if you didn't know that Elaine's words of years ago still hold immense power over him: "It's all *your* fault."

A tragic story? Yes and no. Elaine may have to scrape the bottom of the proverbial barrel before she releases the bitterness and hatred from her heart. The Lord Jesus is merciful to all those who call upon Him. Even though Elaine punishes herself daily, God loves her.

Bobbie has had to work through enormous guilt, anger and hurt, but finally has allowed herself to accept herself in spite of her mother's rejection. She discovered the power of the words, "Though your father and mother reject you, the

Lord will lift you up and never ever release you from the palm of His hand."

I realize I haven't said a lot about the boys in this story because I've wanted to focus on the mother and daughter; but they, too, had to work on their feelings and emotions regarding their mother's rejection of them. They, too, felt if they had been better human beings, things could have been different. Perhaps all their parents' problems were *their* fault. Maybe they never should have left home. And maybe they were just losers like their dad had been. Maybe all women were manipulative, crafty and mean underneath. Maybe you just couldn't trust anybody.

But those feelings were expressed and examined through counseling, prayer, and constant loving communication with their father and sister. Mother wasn't there, but they had to go on. It wasn't their fault that Mother wasn't there.

None of us wants to wind up miserable and lonely like Elaine. Or wounded and suffering with feelings of guilt like the others in this family. Maybe you think this story is an extreme case; after all, Elaine had been a Bible study leader, active in the church, a Christian. It's important to realize that we essentially choose our own destiny. Elaine used the Lord Jesus to justify her own self-righteousness and self-proclaimed piety. She lacked the spiritual depth to bend to hear from Him, to be reproved and corrected. Leaders *must* have a teachable spirit.

All of us are prideful at times, and as mothers it's possible to think we do a far better job of mothering than others. We can boast to ourselves about how clean we keep our bathrooms, how much more we sacrifice for our children than other mothers do, how great we are at cooking, carpooling, or folding towels for the linen closet. But in reality, most of us share the same aspirations and dreams.

We all want our daughters to be happy and healthy, blessed and loved for the whole world to see. And then, regardless of their fame and success, we unrealistically demand that they always remain fiercely and totally loyal and dedicated to the most important human who will ever enter their life—Mom.

To get to the practicality part, we grow with our daughters, we teach them and we learn from them. We learn to be open enough to admit errors when we see them in ourselves. We can say "I'm sorry" and "I love you" as often as we say, "Close the door behind you," and "Good grief, how many times are you going to pierce your ears?"

Rules for Avoiding Tragic Mistakes:

1. Don't be afraid to be imperfect.
2. Give kisses and hugs and words of love and encouragement continually.
3. Realize you are precious to God and don't have to work to gain His approval.
4. Tell yourself daily that God actually likes you so that you will be more aware that He likes your family, too.
5. Remove the demands you have on others to be perfect and exactly as you want them to be and act.
6. Don't be afraid to express your needs and wants such as saying to your daughter, "I need a hug." Or, "Will you please tell me you love me right now?" Or, "Is there anything about me that annoys you or that you think I should change?"
7. Teach yourself to laugh and laugh often. Read funny books, see funny movies, look for humor in your day. And then share these fun moments with your loved ones. Research has shown that people who can laugh together remain closer and desire one another's company more.
8. Be flexible. Be ready to change, to grow, to admit error. Do not be afraid of change.

Don't do this and don't do that
Are the words I hear all day;
No to that and no-no to this,
That's all my parents can say.
Why don't they ever say yes to me,
When will I ever be free?
They may think they're helping
     me grow
With all of this discipline now,
But I hate to be told what to do,
     where to go;
When will they stop saying no!

DISCIPLINE DOESN'T HAVE TO BE PAINFUL

CHAPTER THIRTEEN

Elaine's refusal to change, to bend and to grow cost her a home and family. She could not accept failure as a natural experience in life. To her, it was an overwhelming horror to be avoided. In doing so, she accomplished that which she feared and failed. Pride and fear of being proven wrong or imperfect can rob us of the very thing we crave—acceptance. She longed for approval over and above intimacy. Losing husband, family and home she attributes even to this day to their craven evils.

I've talked about being friends with your teenager, but there are some prerequisites for this development in the mother-daughter relationship. One is the ability of the daughter to handle responsibility. Another is the ability of the mother to *allow* her daughter to handle responsibility, and a third is a mutual sense of respect, trust and integrity.

A small child may have a lot of wonderful attributes, but integrity isn't usually one of them—yet. When my daughters were small I expected them to obey their mother, perform the tasks assigned them, and they did these things not out of a sense of responsibility and integrity, but out of a desire to earn points on their behavior charts plus a healthy

144 ■ Mothers & Daughters

reverence for punishment. The more they did those behaviors that were acceptable and good, the more they learned
the good feelings associated with a job well done. They
learned to appreciate the rewards of obedience, and they
learned that trust is a good thing. They learned parental
respect and therefore self-respect.

There is some controversy over "the rod" in the Bible
verse, "Spare the rod and spoil the child." Parents must ask
themselves, "Is hitting a child always the best rod?" This
question must be faced square-on without hypocrisy. The
parents must examine their motives for hitting, beating,
whipping and physically hurting their child. Answers such
as "My daddy whupped me, so I'll whupp my kid" are not
good enough reason to hurt a child. The parent must ask,
"Is there another form of punishment that will be more
effective and easier on us all?"

It's amazing that a parent will become irate when his
child strikes another child when that parent hits the child
all the time! Parents call this violence "discipline." A mother
or father will sermonize on the sin of hurting another human
being, but that same parent will hit that same child and
excuse the act by calling it the biblical "rod." These acts of
overt anger do far more harm than good. Even more scary
is the parent who, with placid face and calm voice, tells the
child, "It's time for your beating," in much the same man-
ner as when announcing, "It's time for your ice cream." No
wonder so many grown-ups lead empty, undisciplined lives.
We learn young that discipline means pain. Bad pain.

It's a far better thing to warn the child ahead of time by
telling her, "This is what will happen if you break the rule.
You will sit in the corner for one whole hour." (Or whatever
punishment is reasonable. Maybe it will be no TV for the
night or no use of the telephone for a whole day.

Reasonable Punishment

I do not think a reasonable punishment for any infraction
merits grounding a child for long periods of time. A pun-

ishment such as grounding a child, say, for two or three months is usually a sentence passed in a moment of the parent's anger. The only punishment worse is hitting.

The disciplinarian in my house was my father. He may have gone overboard on this calling, and for the most part, just the sound of his voice was enough to keep me in line. When he said sit down and be quiet, let me tell you, wild horses couldn't have gotten me to move. I *froze* in place.

My mother's best punishment was to sit me on a chair in the dining room by the wall. I dreaded that chair. "Do you want to sit on the chair?" was reminder enough for me to do what was expected of me immediately.

I know plenty of people who were never spanked as children, never severely punished; they endured no long-term grounding; no shrieking rages were vented at them, and yet they managed to grow up to lead useful, happy, productive lives! For the most part, I don't think parents discipline their children because they are so concerned how the child will turn out.

I knew that behind the dark brooding eyes of my father there was a terrible force bigger than I. His very presence seemed to command subservience. When I was very small he was loving, fun, sweet and even cuddly, but after I grew out of my early "adorable little girl" years, the hugs and kisses stopped and out came the rules and regulations. From infancy until puberty my father was my hero and joy, and then it all changed when, as my grandmother said, I "got a mind of my own." Still, my father was the undisputed authority and last word in the house. I remember once begging him if I could go to a certain school function. I pleaded, "Please, Dad, everyone is going!"

"Wrong," he said coolly. "*You're* not." And nothing short of a nuclear holocaust would have gotten him to change his mind. In all my life I never knew him to alter a no—not a hair, not a jot, not a bit.

The arduous, not always rewarding, vigorous discipline

I live with today I owe, in part, to my father. It is both good and bad because my father hit hard. I remember once when he hit me on the head so hard that I prayed I would still be able to think clearly later on. I thought he had broken my brain.

This was discipline learned in pain and fear, but today the fear is gone. My brain seems to function OK, I'm a fairly disciplined person, and before my father died, we had become quite close. He certainly taught me the finer points of discipline, and today it is not difficult for me to say no to myself, to go without, to work while the rest of the world is outside playing, and to fulfill promises.

I can say "it is well with my soul" even when I feel left out or unappreciated. My father was strict, and often hit too hard, but his lessons of discipline were formed in me. It may not have been the best way to learn, but I did learn a few lasting lessons. I remember refusing to cower when he struck, and I forced myself not to cry or let him see my tears. It was my small effort at maintaining dignity or a sense of pride. Many times now I observe women as they cower like helpless, frightened children wailing in fear and pain as the world beats at their heads.

My father worked ten- and twelve-hour days on the railroad and often into the wee hours of the morning in the cold, rain, and heat. I knew his life wasn't an easy one, and my mother instilled in us children great respect for him. She often reminded us of his faithfulness and how hard he worked to clothe and feed his family. If he was hard on his family, he was harder on himself.

My mother was the compassionate one, the listener, and she gave me a sense of worth and purpose. They were a good team, my mother and father. But this brings us to another problem.

What do you do if you're the soft-spoken, gentle mom who finds it difficult to so much as slap a mosquito, and your husband is the punitive, hit-'em-over-the-head type man who buys a metal ruler with sharp edges to enforce his authority with the children?

The first thing to remember is that spanking won't warp your child's mind. Beating a child in anger is another thing. Never hit your child in anger. If you're the mother and your husband hits in anger, it's important to talk to him about it. Perhaps have him seek help to learn methods of dealing with and understanding his anger.

Sit down together as parents and discuss boundaries you are going to set for your children. Agree on these without the children present. Never argue about the children in front of them.

When children know the rules and what is expected of them, they gain a sense of structure and confidence. They know both parents uphold the rules and administer punishment. Studies have shown permissiveness is not as conducive to healthy growth as teaching boundaries, discipline and self-control.

I like what Dr. Joseph Procaccini and Mark Kiefaber say about styles of parenting. In their research they found that there are two basic styles of parenting. I'd like to share these two types and modify them somewhat. The two styles are *Controller* and *Developer*.[1] (We talk about the Controller a lot in this book.)

Most parents aren't totally one or the other type, but fall somewhere along a continuum. Procaccini and Kiefaber give a little test to use in order to see what style parent we are. I've used it as a model for the following Parenting Style test.

---

[1]Dr. Joseph Procaccini and Mark Kiefaber, *Parent Burn-Out* (New York: Doubleday and Co., 1983).

Directions: Indicate your level of agreement or disagreement by using the rating scale. 1 is for emphatic disagree, 2 is slightly less emphatic, 3 is middle of the road. 4 is agree but not emphatically, 5 is maximum agree.

1	2	3	4	5
I Disagree Fully			I Agree Fully	

_____ 1. Family customs should keep up with the times.

_____ 2. Children should naturally try to do what is right.

_____ 3. Parents should try to explain reasons behind their decisions.

_____ 4. Children should gradually be allowed to make their own decisions.

_____ 5. Peer pressure is often beneficial for children.

_____ 6. Venturing out into the world is an opportunity children need.

_____ 7. Once your children are on their own, your role as a parent changes in many rewarding ways.

_____ 8. Worrying about your children won't do them any good.

_____ 9. Children should develop their own relationship with the Lord.

_____10. It's enjoyable to include children in adult conversation.

_____11. There are better ways of disciplining children than spanking.

_____12. Most children will naturally use their potential.

Scoring Key: Add up total points and determine your parenting style by using the key below:

12–18 Super Controller and Minimal Developer
19–30 High Controller and Low Developer
31–41 Moderate Controller and Moderate Developer
42–53 Low Controller and High Developer
54–60 Minimal Controller and Super Developer

A Controller is never a happy person. To the controlling person, the world is a hard, cruel place and people are always failing them. The reason is, the world doesn't easily allow itself to be controlled. The controlling Christian is usually a dogmatic, hard, demanding one who shows little mercy to others. As a parent, the Controller is dogmatic, overly protective, strictly structured, directive and inflexible.

The Developer, on the other hand, is more democratic, values the children as individuals, enjoys their curiosity, is not afraid of change.

Controller:	Developer:
Sees children as extension of himself.	Sees children as individuals.
Hates to be wrong.	Learns by mistakes.
Demands obedience.	Is a good listener.
Displays temper and anger by hitting, screaming, or by cold silence.	Is willing to talk about bad feelings.
Demands perfection.	Is tolerant of imperfection.
Mistrusts most people.	Likes people.
Resents children's curiosity.	Sees hardship and diversity as a chance to grow.

On the one hand, the parents must control their children's behavior if they are not to hurt themselves and if certain goals are to be achieved. On the other hand, children must be allowed to develop self-direction and autonomy. Many parenting-style problems originate from either a lack of appreciation of or a simplistic approach to this dilemma. Christians tend to oversimplify by stating a rule and molding it in steel out of fear of losing authority and control.

There is a time to bend and a time to be like steel. Elaine, in our previous chapter, didn't understand this distinction. Rules regarding drugs, sex, obeying the law, lying are unchangeable. Sin can never be anything but sin. There's no bending. On matters such as being allowed to stay out a little later on certain occasions, skipping the dishes, getting her ears pierced or having a friend stay over on a school night—these are "bendable" situations. And to be discussed and agreed upon by both parents when the children aren't around.

If you scored 37 on the Parenting Style test, that's pretty good. You want to be a little of the Controller and Developer to have balance. If you're 100% Controller, you're trying too hard to keep your children on the right course. (Right course to a mother always means the course she thinks is right.)

But you don't want to be a 100% Developer either, because this puts you in the passive wimp category. You'll be raising children in a permissive ungodly atmosphere without any integrity building guidelines for them to follow. As your child grows older, however, you become more of a Developer and you can begin to enjoy the fruits of your discipline.

There is another kind of punishment some parents resort to and it is a close relative of the whip. It's called silence. The icy stare. The stiff-jawed refusal to communicate. "What's wrong, Mom?" is assaulted with a glare and a tight lip. "Nothing" may be the hissed retort, which really means, "You ought to know what's wrong, you insolent cur, you." Someone once said that most of us become parents long before we have stopped being children, but somewhere in our lives we must at least consider that this world wasn't formed for our convenience. I agree with Margaret Mead, who said we must have a place where children can have a whole group of adults they can trust. This trust begins with parents.

Integrity always includes discipline. And to discipline with integrity is to give to our children a precious gift. Perhaps we can raise a generation of people who can learn self-denial and how to work long and hard without complaint.

Discipline is crucial to our well-being. Show me a person

without the ability to discipline him or herself, to sacrifice, to lay him or herself on the altar for the Master's use, and I'll show you a frustrated and unhappy person. We teach our children to love discipline or to hate it. David said, "Oh, how I love Thy law!" and we can teach our daughters that law is good and God's law is beautiful. It protects us, keeps us safe, blesses us and teaches us the ways of righteousness, peace and joy in the Holy Spirit. The benefits of discipline and obedience to His Word far outweigh any other benefit life may offer.

We can learn this when we are young. God bless the child who does.

Mamma, I dreamed I could do anything and be anything I want—is that true?

—*Five-year-old Cancer Victim*

THE DREAM-MAKER

CHAPTER FOURTEEN

When we are young Mom is our primary caretaker. She doesn't necessarily have to be our natural birth mother, just as long as we're mothered by somebody. Sometimes an uncle has to be the mother or a baby-sitter, a grandparent, a nanny or a dad. But mothering, meaning nurturing, feeding, caring for, providing the essentials, is vital to our well-being in our early years and affects the rest of our lives.

Becoming independent, both within and without, is a process. Our dreams may be loftier than our inner development can manage. Daring to dream requires inner development as well as increased outer skills of life.

Inner skills are learned. They are the skills that allow us to dream and give us permission to be as great as we want to be; to do wonderful feats and exploits, to hear the voice and the call of God on our lives. When we respond only to an inner drive for excellence, we are not blessed with God's perfect guidance and assurance of being in His will.

Inner skills begin with a relationship with our God. He is Lord of dreams, the Great Dream-Maker. To come to know Him intimately is to come to know ourselves.

He teaches us that we are in charge of our dreams. And we are responsible for our feelings, our dedication to the dream.

We are not dependent upon others for approval and for a

sense of our own value. He has loved us with an everlasting love, and of this we are confident. We learn these things young; we reinforce them gradually as we grow. Women of God need to have a dream; we need to follow that dream, need to love the Dream-Maker.

Hearing the voice of the Dream-Maker is the calling of every mom and the joy of every little girl. These are the skills:

> I am me
> And that is a very good thing to be.
>
> You are you
> And that is a very good thing to be.
>
> Together we are valuable and special
> And apart we are valuable and special too.

My daughter Christa had a dream. She wanted to run. But long before that, when she was about six months old, she was lying in her crib playing with her Busy Box when I noticed something strange about her feet. Her tiny toes, smaller than peas, feet as soft and fat as two ripe kiwi fruit didn't look quite right. Her father's feet were crooked and flat. Would hers be?

For months I said nothing, only prayed. Pediatricians assured me it was only baby fat that made her feet look so odd. Later, orthopedists told me that nothing could be done until she started walking. She didn't walk for sixteen months, and then only cautiously on the outside edges of her feet. We knew. We understood. This perfect baby had deformed feet.

So Christa moved through childhood in special shoes. The orthopedists in New York, Chicago, Minneapolis, and even a famous surgeon at Scripps in La Jolla, California, told us nothing could be done until her bones stopped growing. I began, routinely, holding her feet in my two hands and blessing them. Year after year.

"How beautiful upon the mountain are the feet of the little girl who brings good news. . . ."

"Dear Jesus, thank you for healing my feet. . . ."

She rarely complained until the sixth grade when she became disgruntled that her feet didn't look like everybody else's feet. And she wanted to wear normal shoes, but she hobbled along on twisted toes, blisters and growing bunions. One day she muttered angrily, "Mom, I have ugly feet."

I said, "Nothing formed by God is ugly."

"Did God make my feet like this?"

"Everything you are, every hair on your head, every pore and cell of your body belongs to Him. He doesn't call your feet ugly; He calls them blessed."

The surgeon at Scripps told her, "With feet like yours, you'd make a good swimmer. Try swimming." We left his office that day embarrassed and enraged. Was my daughter a duck?

"Your feet are blessed, Christa," I said.

I have always loved fitness, sports, exercise, dance. I'm an outdoor person with an indoor life. I looked at my daughters who had before them opportunities to climb the high Sierras, dance, win at tennis, ski, teach aerobics, run marathons . . .

Run marathons. Christa was in high school when she decided to be a cross-country runner. With her deformed, blessed feet.

"Teach me, Mom," she said. "Be my trainer."

So down to the track we went. "Come on, Christa, push off the back foot, easy, easy . . ."

My daughter—scrawny, hobbling, hurting—said, "Mom, I don't think I can do it."

"Come on, Christa, *I can do all things through Christ who strengtheneth me.*"

The next day, around the track again. And again the day after. Tears streaming down her cheeks, reeling, working at gaining body alignment, "I can do all things through Christ who strengtheneth me."

Then she's passing me, around the track through the mud, the grasses, on the gravel, the asphalt, up hills, down hills. Building strength. Building muscle and endurance. "I can do all things through Christ. . . ."

We did interval training. She ran hard one day, easier the next. She made the cross-country team at her school. And when the coach took the team on a mountain climbing trip, Christa climbed the mountain. Blisters, bandages, special shoes, red-inflamed bunions, burning toes, she did it.

"Are you sure this is what you want, Christa?"

"I'm sure."

Then came the first competitive race. What a day. Nervous. Excited. Last on the team. The first mile went easy, smooth. Then she stepped in a hole, turned her ankle and fractured her foot. So she was in a cast up to her knee and she couldn't train and she couldn't run. But when the cast came off she trained again. "Easy, easy, Christa . . . Glide gently, keep your pace."

"I can do all things through Christ. . . ."

"I *want* to run, Mom." It was her dream.

The following year she was back on the team and off to another competitive race. Not even a mile completed and the foot twisted, broke, and down she went. This time she was carried to the hospital on a stretcher, and in a cast for two months.

For years I had prayed for a miracle. I requested prayer for my girl's feet at prayer meetings and Bible studies. I blessed her feet, massaged them, soaked them in salts, wrapped them, loved them. I came to the realization that my trust and hope could not lie in God's answering prayer *my* way. I had to be at peace, trusting in His perfect character and will above my own desires.

By the time Christa was nineteen years old, her toes were mashed together like pressed macaroni. They pointed outward at 45 degree angles. The bunions were like golf balls. And then came the day when she would lie flat on a gurney, brown eyes dimmed, while being wheeled into the operating room for the surgery that would make her feet normal.

Here's another moment nobody prepares a mother for. I was alone, waiting there in the hallway while they broke up, cut up, sawed and wired her bones together. Some people said, "Good luck." Others said, "I'll be praying for you." And some said, "Oh, I know someone who had their feet straightened and it left them worse than before. Crippled them right up. Pathetic."

The nurses were kind to my girl in the hospital. They talked to her, plumped her pillows, were right on time with the pain medication. And her doctor was right there—concerned, caring, even available in the wee hours of the morning when she cried out in disquieting pain.

Together, we read the words from Isa. 48:10: "I have chosen thee in the furnace of affliction." We pondered these words together, my daughter and I, and we asked ourselves if we are truly confident of His sure promise to His chosen ones in a time of intense pain.

The promise to keep us in the palm of His hand. Never forsaking us, giving us strength in time of need, lifting us higher, ever present in time of need. Our rock and our fortress, our strength and our redeemer. "He redeems me from the fear of suffering. . . ."

"In the furnace of affliction," my daughter explained to me, "I can learn to be more like Him."

But could I?

Once home again, I wheeled this brown-eyed child outside every day, down the sloping sidewalk, up rutted streets in her bandaged feet and wheelchair. My girlfriend, Gene, named her Miracle Feet. After nineteen years.

God's furnace can make us beautiful if we hold still while we're in it. How beautiful upon the mountain are the feet of her who brings good news. . . .

Today, she runs and she runs without pain, without tears. She had a dream and the Dream-Maker made it come true.

My children's lives teach me about the faithfulness of God, and I learn more about independence as I watch them reaching for it and succeeding.

And in trusting Him, I can let go. The Dream-Maker shows me how.

. . . And soon the parents know
the privilege given
In caring for their gift from
heaven;
Their precious charge, so meek
and mild,
Is heaven's very special child.

—*Edna Massimilla*

HEAVEN'S SPECIAL CHILD

CHAPTER FIFTEEN

Every woman who becomes pregnant dreams, hopes and prays that she will bear a perfect child. Upon giving birth, she sighs in relief at the first small cries from tiny, healthy lungs, she counts the toes and fingers, runs her hands over every inch of this amazing little body, waiting for the doctor to pronounce the long-awaited verdict: "You have a healthy, perfect baby."

And yet we know that not every mother hears those words. And as children grow, eyes, legs, muscles, nerve-endings sometimes do not do exactly what they were created to do. Having had a child who suffered, I know what fears and frustrations can play upon your spirit, weighing it down. I know the negative, life-draining thoughts that can come to wring joy from life.

But I know that, in the Spirit of God, there can be real victory.

Christa was confined to a wheelchair for two months. It was a big day for us when she took her first steps again, when her feet withstood the weight of her body, when her legs held her up and when all of the muscles, tendons, ligaments and bones in her feet, legs and spine functioned normally. She could walk again.

There are those who are limited to the space of their wheelchairs far longer. Some their entire lives. Their legs never do get better, their feet never do recover and they never do run or walk or stand again.

Sharon is a woman who is called "handicapped"—and she is a wife, mother of three grown children, business-woman and co-owner of a home-based consulting and business management company, an active church worker, secretary and editor and volunteer for the Post Polio Network, full-time secretary and administrative assistant in a Christian ministry organization, and active in helping others through her seemingly effortless giving, sharing and assisting anyone who comes her way in need. Yet Sharon has not walked in thirty-eight years.

Handicapped: It means somebody who is different. Sharon is physically handicapped. Not mentally, not emotionally. She has feelings like most people; she laughs, cries, eats, dresses and brushes her teeth in the morning like most people. Her body has feeling, normal bladder and bowel control, normal sex drive; she has borne children; she thinks, dreams, hurts, prays.

Sharon is well aware of the word *handicapped*. When her children were in elementary school, she was the only parent at the PTA meetings in a wheelchair, the only mother who watched her son play Little League baseball with binoculars from the car because her wheelchair couldn't get through the sand and dirt to the field; the only mother who couldn't sit with her children at the theater or other special events because she had to sit in the section for the handicapped. There were, and still are the times when Sharon can't get into her car because someone else parks too close to hers, blocking her chances of getting the door open to hoist her wheelchair and herself inside. And any able-bodied mother can take her child to the restroom when the occasion warrants. Sharon knows what it is like to stare at a toilet and not be able to reach it or help her child use it.

This one simple ability of balancing unsupported and upright on two feet is enough to include or separate us from the world we are born into, enough to open the gates of opportunity to us or alienate us from any possibility of transcending the limitations of our braces, crutches, wheelchair or bed.

Sharon was bright as a child, a child who loved to learn. She had a high IQ, the same as her able-bodied twin brother. But getting to school, to her classroom and into her desk was a far greater challenge than the schoolwork. And the other kids weren't always kind. With her lifeless legs in braces, she struggled about on crutches, through the hallways, up and down the stairs.

"I was so self-conscious," she says, "because my rear end stuck out and my dresses all went up in the back and hung down in the front and it was hard to carry books and manage the crutches at the same time. So I would fall down."

A bright child, a child who loved to learn—sprawled across the floor, books and papers splattered, a skinned knee, wounded pride, and then an impertinent classmate's foot gives a kick, and accompanied by choruses of laughter, her crutches go flying out of her reach.

There was the time a snake was put in her desk and she couldn't jump out of the seat. Another time when class was over, she reached for her crutches at the side of her desk and they were gone. The laughter. Someone had taken her legs and hidden them.

These experiences define a handicap.

Sharon contracted the polio virus in 1949. That year 47,000 polio-stricken children suffered along with her. Sharon's mother says the polio wards in hospitals were like living hells as sounds of screaming, moaning youngsters filled the halls. The pain this virus inflicted on the little victims' bodies was devastating. Helpless parents could only look on and try despairingly to comfort their children. In 1952 there were 57,879 cases of poliomyelitis reported.

And then in 1955 the Salk vaccine. Sharon rejoiced, knowing there would be fewer and fewer cases of the disease she thought had taken away her dignity.

But dignity and integrity are not attributes we're born with. They're developed. God gives us, when we reach toward Him, the awareness that, "Because *He* is, I am." And you can follow that with, "Because I am, and because *He* accepts me, I accept me." These attitudes and way of life are gained only through deep self-searching, awareness and acceptance. In other words, we *learn* integrity. The school of suffering can help us to this end. In alienation and pain, God is there pulling us gently up out of the sorrows of the heart into our truer selves.

> For Thou didst form my inward parts;
> Thou didst weave me in my mother's womb.
> I will give thanks to Thee, for I am fearfully and
>   wonderfully made;
> Wonderful are Thy works,
> And my soul knows it very well. (Ps. 139:13, 14)

Any child's struggle for integrity is painstaking. Part of its nature is death to self and self-will. Another ingredient is respect for time. Sharon's mother assured her, "The hard times will end—it'll be OK."

Throughout her illness and in the ensuing years, Sharon came to depend on her mother to the point where she believed there could be no life without her. Her mother exercised her legs and turned their New Jersey basement into a physical therapy rehab center complete with hot water pool and gym. This woman who exercised her, encouraged her, helped her, remained at her side night and day became Sharon's connection to the real world.

But her mother didn't accept her daughter's inability to walk. Sharon longed to have a wheelchair so it would be faster getting around school and so she wouldn't fall down, but her mother wanted her to *walk*. She was eager to grab onto the slightest hope for her child; she took Sharon to doctors, specialists and clinics across the country, seeking miracle cures and subjecting the child to injections, potions, medications, diets and exercises in the futile hope that she would one day be "normal" again.

It would be many years before Sharon realized she already was normal.

"I had to learn to accept myself as I was," Sharon says. "One day I couldn't stand any more of these cures. I broke down in tears and begged my mother not to take me for any more tests, or injections, or muscle and nerve response tests, or orange juice mixed with a ton of vitamins and magic cures. No more doctors. I pleaded with her to accept me as I was. I felt she wouldn't ever really love me unless I could walk. I felt so rejected by the world, by life.

"My mother is a sensitive and loving person and I can understand her pain now. But I couldn't understand it back then. I was only aware of my *own* pain. She just wanted the best for me and, to her, the best would be my total healing and being able to walk again.

"All the personal suffering and sacrifice my mother went through for me just meant that in order to be truly loved you had to be able-bodied. It seemed to me that walking was my mother's main dream for me. It was awful knowing what a disappointment I must have been to her."

"Please, Mom. Please, please accept me as I am!"

One day, Sharon heard of a group of handicapped people who met to socialize and *dance* every week, and so her mother drove her to the meeting one night. It became the bright light of Sharon's life. She had not known any handicapped people before this, had never socialized with other people who were paraplegic or quadriplegic or post-polio victims. This was her chance to fit in socially. She learned to dance in a wheelchair and with great exuberance and delight she learned to do wheelies, to twirl and rock and enjoy the rhythm of the music with her body just like able-

bodied people did. She became a member of the "Wheela-
cade" and along with a team of other talented wheelchair
dancers, performed all over the state of California.

"For the first time, I was having the time of my life. I
could show the kids at school the technique I learned balancing the wheelchair on its back wheels. I thought maybe
now they wouldn't think I was so different, after all."

Her mother will tell you, a special child like Sharon is a
gift from God. She gives you far more than is estimable.
This poem, which reads in part expresses it:

> And soon [the parents] know the privilege given
> In caring for their gift from heaven;
> Their precious charge, so meek and mild,
> Is heaven's very special child.

Once independent of her mother's protection and care,
she was able to shed the braces and the crutches, which had
become more and more difficult and unmanageable for her.
Scoliosis and lordosis of the spine were causing the curve at
her waist to push the spine inward toward her stomach. At
last she was allowed to maneuver around in the comparative
comfort of a wheelchair.

Becoming truly independent is only possible when self-
esteem is intact; otherwise breaking the bonds of family ties
is an act of rebellion or running away from responsibility.
Sharon was married, gave birth to two boys, and fifteen years
later, became the foster mother to a daughter.

In the hospital after giving birth to her first child, she
examined his tiny body, and holding her baby with the perfect body and strong perfect little legs and feet, something
from deep within her leaped into him and forever after each
time this child walked, she walked too.

Today, Sharon says, "Twenty-five years ago at the time
of my first child's birth, you didn't see wheelchairs in thea-
ters and restaurants. Shopping was nearly impossible. When
my children were babies, like six months and a year-and-a-
half old, just going to the store for milk was a procedure

that could take half a day. I had to carry both children on my lap to the car. David would hop into his little car seat in the back, I'd lay the baby down on the floor of the car, lift myself onto the seat, fold my wheelchair, and pull it into the backseat. Then I'd slide over to the driver's seat, pick the baby up off the floor, strap him in the passenger seat and off we'd go. God forbid if I forgot anything."

But if getting there was the only problem, it would have been easy, says Sharon. There were the other obstacles—like finding handicapped parking available and then she'd have the task of finding a space that allowed enough room for a wheelchair to get through. Then there were the problems of curbs or traffic, and finally swinging, revolving or narrow doors. Rain presented another set of difficulties. Crowds another.

Being a mother in a wheelchair is just like being a mother not in a wheelchair (except for not being able to take the children shopping in a hurry, and except for not running after them when they've been naughty, and not being able to get up stairs, and not being able to sit with them at the circus or basketball and football games, and not being able to ride the rides at the fair, and having to crawl on the floor dragging her legs behind her if the wheelchair isn't nearby, and being unable to reach high places, and getting stuck in crooked hallways, and not being able to go certain places because of narrow access, and except for not being able to park the car if the handicap parking spaces are taken, and being either pitied or patronized, ignored or indulged, and for lack of socialization and inclusion in normal society—except for these few inconveniences plus many not named, the mother in the wheelchair is just like any other mother).

Isn't God a God of healing? Doesn't it clearly say in Isaiah 53 He healeth "all our diseases"? Doesn't the Bible tell us He comes with healing in His wings, and doesn't it say ask and we receive? Why does heaven's special child not receive a healing? Why does God not miraculously touch her lifeless legs and restore their muscle and strength? Nothing is impossible to Him, after all. Is her faith lacking? The Lord has told us without faith it's impossible to please Him, but Sharon and thousands of others who are sick or handicapped do have faith. Years of prayer. Tears, pleadings in the night hours, worn and calloused knees, hounding the gates of glory for mercy.

When will we grow up and accept the call of God to honor Him in all things? When will we start loving and accepting one another? Why can we not see God in the wheelchair as well as on a church platform? Is He not Lord of *all*? And does this not mean Lord of the brace, the surgery, the cast, the crutch, the medication, the wheelchair?

No matter how dark the darkness, finding Christ requires looking hard. Someone once told me they looked for Christ everywhere and couldn't find Him. They looked in the gutter, in the mud, in the slow-moving sand, and they couldn't find Him. I said, "But you didn't look up."

If we want to find Christ, we must look up. Beyond people—even religious ones. And when we do, we elevate our own vantage points. We see clearer. And from this new perspective, with our eyes and hearts fixed ahead and upward where we expect to find glory, we at last distinguish His face. We gaze into the perfect reality of Him, His presence, His love, and we become transfixed in wonder. Because there, in the center of His image, we see ourselves. Our true selves.

In Him we become our true selves.

Because He is, I am.

Sharon hasn't walked in thirty-eight years, but she discovered God. Despite bitterness and anger, she looked up. She had made a practice of feeling hurt, misunderstood, unlovable and alone, and she must daily choose to meet Him on His terms. Those terms are always ensconced in love. God is not intimidated by our responses to pain. He is not rendered helpless by our helplessness. He is not so small,

nor His arm so short that He cannot reach out and save us
from the monsters of self-destruction.

> Though I walk in the midst of trouble, Thou wilt
> revive me;
> Thou wilt stretch forth Thy hand against the wrath of
> my enemies,
> And Thy right hand will save me.
> The Lord will accomplish what concerns me;
> Thy lovingkindness, O Lord, is everlasting.
>
> (Ps. 138:7, 8)

When her children were young, they scattered their toys
only at the *edges* of the rooms and along the walls. These,
her babies, whom nobody could take from her, these babies
were hers. Hers. They made a path for her. They knew.
They understood.

And they grew up. Her foster daughter became her
friend, her darling friend who shopped with her, talked for
hours at the dining room table, helped her, loved her. "Oh,
don't feel sorry for my mom. She may be in a wheelchair,
but believe me, she's just fine."

And her sons: "When anybody says 'poor Sharon,' I just
tell them right off, our mom can take care of herself; she's
got more guts than you think. She's a fighter and a do-er.
She's our example.

"Mom has great faith in God. And she has a heart of
gold. She has prayed for us kids every day of our lives since
we were born. One time she got us together and asked us if
we were embarrassed to have a *handicapped* mother. We
wanted to laugh out loud. Handicapped. She keeps the
house cleaner than any able-bodied mother we know. And
she's *always* there for us. She loves us unconditionally even
when we pull some bad stuff.

"If one of us were to wake her up at 3 a.m. and say,
'Mom, would you type this paper for me?' Or,' Mom, would
you help me out with a problem I have?' she'd get right out
of bed and help us. That's the kind of mom we have.

"To us she's just plain Mom. And that's special."

"They made a path for me. . . ."

She's endured twenty-three surgeries, and once had to have carpotunnel surgery on her hands when she couldn't cut her meat or button her shirt or open a door, and she has experiences other mothers don't have. She has fallen out of her chair on streets and in parking lots to the shock and bewilderment of passers-by; she's been invited to a baby shower and excitedly bought and wrapped the gift, dressed and driven to the house only to watch from outside and then have to drive home again because nobody told her about the four steps leading up to the front door.

"I want to tell you something, Marie," says Sharon. "A person who doesn't go through something is a weak person. I don't want my children to say their mother is a weak person. I want them to see what Jesus can do for a person who loves Him."

I will give thanks to Thee, for I am fearfully and wonderfully made.

"Don't feel sorry for my mom. She may be in a wheelchair but she's just fine."

"Please . . . accept me as I am. . . ."

"To us, she's just plain Mom, and that's special."

Jesus said to them, My food [nourishment] is to do the will [pleasure] of Him Who sent Me and to accomplish and completely finish His work.

—John 4:34, The Amplified Bible

LETTING GO

CHAPTER SIXTEEN

Many mothers, like Sharon's mother, can become dependent upon their daughter's dependency. It was not an easy task for Sharon's mother to give up her role as primary caretaker to her daughter. When Sharon married Rick, a handsome, strong, and able-bodied man, it was a serious adjustment for her mother.

What does a woman do when her life's work ends and she still has half her life to live? Gail Sheehy, author of *Passages*, said, "No one tells girls that motherhood is only half a 'lifework.' " Mothers expect to go on mothering until kingdom come. "My little girl may be grown up and on her own, but she'll always be my baby" may be a quaint thought and one I personally hold dear to my heart, but we have to look at it with the harsh, unfiltered eyes of truth.

Little girls who grow up don't need Mommy. Our needs change.

I'm a little girl who grew up, somebody's one-time baby and daughter, but what I need most now is not Mommy or a Fantasy Mom, but a friend and a strong role model. We each need to draw strength from the wisdom and strength of the older women of God who have blazed a trail for us younger ones to follow.

In my studies and research of familial relationships, I discovered an abundance of mommies out there looking for someone to coddle to their bosoms and take care of. Some of these women are downright desperate. With the present draught of child-adults—due to a resurgence of great spiritual and psychological awareness and therefore, a mental health boon—there are fewer and fewer baby grown-ups who are willing to be juvenilized. The situation is serious. These professional mommies are reduced to baking cookies for their dogs, knitting sweaters for cats and giving lessons in elocution to their minah birds. They talk back to their television sets and give gifts to the postman and the gardener. They labor daily to maintain approval in non-intimate relationships to keep their giving, mommy status.

When these women do selflessly give to a worthy cause—such as missionary outreach through the church, or serving on a board or teaching a Bible study, or donating to and helping the needy—they are deeply offended when their efforts aren't given due gratitude and attention. ("Shame on you; you didn't say thank you to Mommy. Now, what do you say?")

Letting go is an experience nobody prepares us for. It's a rare mother who is fully prepared for it. Giving up a daughter to marriage, for example, is almost like condoning kidnapping for some mothers. One mother told me, "I can't understand why we have to give up our precious girls to these guys who haven't known them one-eighth the years we have." Another woman told me, "These men our daughters see as knights, heros—these insolent, albeit 'nice enough' fellows can just come along and take away my daughters and then a few years down the line leave them with a couple of kids to raise alone. I already don't trust this one my eldest daughter is engaged to. I almost hate him."

No matter who he is, how terrific, how good, how honest, he is a bum. He comes dashing out of the brush to steal away our precious angel like a thief in the night. Where is justice? What about the lifetime investment in these daughters? The years of sacrifice and nurturing?

A woman whose only child had just announced her engagement said to me, "Are mothers only allowed the right to be of use until the kids say 'I do'? I feel like I'm thrown to the rubble heap, doomed to loneliness, an occasional visit at Christmas and long-distance phone calls.

"Are we left, in our twilight years, to sit by our mailboxes, or with our children's baby books on our laps, reminiscing about the days when we were important and indispensable human beings?"

Nobody prepares us for this. Nobody warns us. Everybody tells us how to raise our kids, but nobody tells us how to say goodbye to them. Nobody tells us about letting go. Lord, help us.

One of the most traumatic days of my life was the day in September when I drove my daughter to college for her first longterm experience away from home. She was accepted at a good Christian college in southern California an hour and a half away. We celebrated—I especially. I was so thrilled for her to be going to college, living in a dorm, the works. We shopped for her new school clothes, linens, towels, and I chirped along happy as could be, proud as Tolstoi after writing *War and Peace*. And then came the day we drove up to the school.

A sunshiny day, the car packed to the sun roof, singing up the highway as we went. I was beaming with delight at having come to one of life's milestones, a veritable "passage," naive as to what lay in wait for me. We hauled her stuff up to her room, we prayed, I helped her unpack, make her bunk bed—oh, the fun of it all. I was sort of like a bouncing clown, pleased with every little detail of the place: the mom who never got to live in a dorm or go away to private college. It was a dream come true. So we kissed and hugged and I bounced back into the empty car—and then it hit me.

My baby had left me. I felt myself decompose. I cried so hard I had to pull off the interstate. I sat on the beach crying and howling and hyper-ventilating, because it hit me that this could be it. The big *it*. In only a matter of minutes she was a resident of a new place where she'd be for four years, after which time she may never come home to live permanently again. I suddenly missed her so intensely, so completely that I was consumed with a sort of grief I'd never known. It spread over me in cold, gray dread that her sounds, her face, her voice, the exhilarating conversations, her laughter, her music . . . were gone.

We called each other daily. Then one day the calls stopped. She was bonded in up there at that school, that place where she belonged, and she was a part of a whole new life. A life without me. And I had to let go.

But letting go takes time.

Prepare for the day your little girl leaves home. Prepare by seeing yourself as a separate entity, an important person in your own right *sans* the title "mother" now. Plan for the day your daughter becomes independent and start imagining your life without the kids around. Think about what you will want to be doing X years from now, whether it's travel, going back to school, switching careers, entering the work force, starting a new ministry, serving the Lord full time, being a short-term missionary; but plan *now*. There *is* life beyond raising children.

My daughter is now in her second year of college and I'm coping. The house still echoes in silence without her sounds. I confess that I still long to look at her face, to hear her voice; I even miss the milk carton she usually leaves on the counter, the lights she forgets to turn off, my best earrings she takes without asking, but I'm coping. I don't call her up and put the dogs on the phone anymore to remind her how we all miss her. And to show you how much I've grown in my letting-go experience, I am even helping and encouraging her with her second summer in Europe as a student missionary.

It's important that we mothers plan for our years beyond raising our children. Letting go of your son, your little boy, can be an even worse trauma. You're the one who raised him, loved him, nursed him, stuck by him, went through all his ups and downs, rebellions, illnesses—and now he leaves you. Your calling as a mother of a son is to bless him and teach him to be a loving, tenderhearted man of God. Then you must let him go. Prepare early.

If the Lord doesn't return for us before it happens, I have to plan for the day when my daughters are completely on their own. I have to see myself ten years from now, twenty, thirty, forty, *fifty* years from now! Beyond that, I'm reasonably sure I will be going back to school for another degree, or falling out of trees like George Bernard Shaw was doing at ninety.

Do you want to create an adult baby? Then hang on to your daughter. Cling to her. Remind her you're the only one who truly loves and understands her. Inform her often how you're the one person on this earth who cares if she eats or not, who worries about her grades in school, who can't sleep if she's not in the house. Do your best to keep her needy and dependent. Always make her bed, do her laundry, run home to make her a sandwich even though you're in the middle of doing something that is important to you. Put your own life on hold, and remind her regularly you don't know where she'd be without you.

Daughters have to take part in this letting-go experience, also. Daughters need to prepare for it, too. Opening a checking account while in high school, getting a drivers license, taking extra classes for extra credit in school to enhance chances of getting into a good college, getting a part-time job, cleaning and cooking without being told—all of these things are important and fun.

Three essential components of self-esteem are agreed upon by most psychologists: First, a feeling of belonging; second, a feeling of being worthwhile; and third, a feeling of being capable. These three needs integrate to form the necessary elements of self-esteem.[1]

The feeling of belonging and being wanted is crucial to our sense of well-being. A Swedish study of 120 children who were unwanted by their parents showed these children to be worse off in every respect in comparison to the control group over a 21-year period. Among the unwanted children, antisocial and criminal behavior, public dependence and psychiatric illness were twice as prevalent. The impulse to violence is high among those who were denied a mother's love and who experienced little humanity at the hands of others.

One young girl in sixth grade confided, "If I hadn't been born, my mother could have been a great scientist. She had to give her career up for me." She felt like an intruder, unwanted and guilty for being.

The daughter learns from the time she is a small child that a feeling of worth and value is associated with "I am good," or "I count for something." Mothers give this feeling to their daughters by wholeheartedly being interested in them and their actions and by giving approval.

"My mother always nags, never approves," a sixteen-year-old girl told me. "I can always hear her voice in the back of my head telling me I didn't do well enough or it's not good enough."

A feeling of capability is so important to self-esteem, a daughter can't leave home without it. I was working with a fourteen-year-old girl not long ago who had developed a learning block. So great was her fear of failure that she wouldn't allow herself to attempt her schoolwork. Her parents were frantic.

Her anxiety started after she returned to school following

---

[1]Fritz Ridenour, *What Teenagers Wish Their Parents Knew About Kids* (Waco, Texas: Word, 1982), quoting Dorothy Briggs, *Your Child's Self-Esteem* (New York: Dolphin Books, 1975), and Maurice Wagner, *The Sensation of Being Somebody* (Grand Rapids: Zondervan Publishing, 1975).

an illness that had kept her home for five days. She was so behind in her work, it seemed impossible to catch up. She flunked quizzes, failed to hand in papers or take exams, skipped classes and finally received "Incompletes" on her report card. When her parents sent her to me for help, she told me she hated school and never wanted to go back.

You could hardly blame the girl. Every minute in the place was painful. The only good times she had were with her friends, getting into trouble. Her feeling of capability had gone down the tubes. Without it she lacked purpose and drive.

Our task was to help her learn to feel good about herself again by giving her small assignments she could accomplish. One day, after she wrote a short paper, for which she was to be rewarded by her parents according to their agreement, I looked at it long and hard and said to her, "You know what? You really write well." I saw her face brighten. "I like what you've written here," I continued. "You've given me something to think about." The next time we were together she showed me a five-page paper she had written, and that was the beginning of her comeback. She finished the year with her class—after some hard work and effort on her part—but much of the credit goes to her parents, who were right there to reward her for completed tasks and assignments and for praising her for a job well done.

I saw her recently and she told me she had decided to be a writer. She belongs, she's worthwhile, she's capable. Therefore, she can see herself fitting into and contributing to an adult world. The future looks friendly, not ominous. That summer she withdrew from the negative, trouble-bound friends she had aligned herself with and began choosing friends with ambitions to match her own.

This daughter is one day going to let go and join the world of other loved, accepted, worthwhile, capable adults who are bringing light to a dark world and hope to an embittered, desolate people.

In letting go, we are really giving our final assent to one another. We are saying our irrevocable, "I approve."

We give to one another the assurance, "You and I were meant to be individuals and to design our own life courses. I am here to bless you, love you, encourage you and stand by you in your choices because I believe in you."

I'd like to give a silken reception to the words of William Arthur Ward:

> The mediocre teacher tells.
> The good teacher explains.
> The superior teacher demonstrates.
> The great teacher inspires.

And only the inspired can inspire others. I can agree with great words of wisdom, but if my own heart is not kindled with life and inspiration, I can't inspire anybody else. I will hunger for another's burning touch of life upon my own. I will be a needy soul, a mommy looking for the poor soul of a baby-adult to make me feel needed, or I will present myself as an adult-baby looking for the world to be my mommy and take care of me.

Deborah, a judge in Israel, a leader and a woman who led an army to victory, sang in glorious exaltation, "I Deborah arose, a mother in Israel. . . ."

In the midst of battle with the powerful enemy, Sisera, Deborah and Barak led 10,000 men into victory as Deborah prayed, "O my soul, march on with strength" (Judg. 5:21).

God responds to such prayers. "The eyes of the Lord move to and fro throughout the earth that He *may strongly support* those whose heart is completely His" (2 Chron. 16:9).

Women of God teach their daughters the ways of wisdom and strength, the ways of courage and holiness, the ways of beauty and victory in Christ.

Because we are the daughters of the Lord.

But then there is the mother who falls short, who disappoints and fails her daughters. In the next chapter we will look at her, this woman we so desperately want to love us, wholly, the Mother Who Isn't.

Some mamas are real ones
And some mamas are make
*   believe ones.*
I'm real and I'm a beautiful
*   princess,*
but nobody knows it. I would
*   give up*
being a beautiful princess
if I could have a real mama.

—Seven-year-old Daughter of
Drug-addicted Mother

THE MOTHER WHO ISN'T

CHAPTER SEVENTEEN

Some little girls grow up without the benefit of loving mothers to guide, nurture and provide for all their emotional and physical needs.

I wrote a book in 1985 called *Forgive Me*, the story of Cathy Crowell Webb who retracted a rape charge that sent an innocent man to prison for six years. It was a news sensation and the story went around the world, causing public outrage and amazement on every continent. All of the major radio and television networks, news services, motion picture companies and international periodicals hounded Cathy for exclusive interviews. Her life after the retraction became a nightmare of reporters, court hearings, lawyer squabbles, financial troubles and public disgrace. Besides this, she was pregnant with her third child and her foster family had disowned her.

How could she, as a sixteen year-old girl, have concocted a false rape and accuse a man she had never even seen before of a crime that never took place? In the time he was imprisoned, she moved out of town, was married and had two children.

How could she live with herself for those six years, knowing that because of her lie an innocent man was locked behind bars? These are the questions the whole world seemed to be asking. *People* magazine voted Cathy one of the Ten Most Fascinating Personalities of the Year.

Cathy's childhood was one of loneliness and alienation. She was taken from her mother when she was three years old and put in the foster care of a stern and ailing seventy-year-old woman whom she learned to call Aunt Nellie. Though she was never beaten or physically abused in her foster home, she was never made to feel that her life was of value. She was tolerated. Again, I recognized the acute mother need unmet.

First the terror, then the nightmares in every crook of a strange new home, then the confusion, the mistrust. Unfamiliar people became Cathy's major caretakers, monoliths she would have hidden behind Mother's legs to keep from facing, if her mother had been there. Then came the hollow, lost feeling, the loneliness. The knowing you've lost something and are guilty. Finally came the questions. The giants of the adult world who made choices for her didn't explain what went wrong. Was she responsible for being here because she was naughty in her real home? Was she being punished? Was it because she wet the bed that night on Lake Shore Drive? . . .

She had heard her mother say she couldn't take it any longer. Had she been a bad girl, too bad to put up with? She still didn't know why her father didn't come to take her home with him, couldn't understand where her mother was. This dilemma, she reasoned, could be only because she was bad . . .

It was Nellie's house, Nellie's table, her pillows and her cookies. They weren't Cathy's—never would be hers, not like a home that had once been hers with all its chairs, bowls and drawers. And Nellie let Cathy know in no uncertain terms that she was there only because of Nellie's big heart.[1]

---

[1]Cathleen Crowell Webb and Marie Chapian, *Forgive Me* (New Jersey: Fleming Revell, 1985, Berkeley Edition, 1986).

Cathy wasn't hugged, praised for doing something well, or told she was a good girl or a pretty girl, and she wasn't encouraged to develop beyond "behaving." She wasn't *mothered*. She was a victim of a rare 100-percent controller-type caretaker. Because of it, she was a lonely, unhappy child who lived in dread and fear and who learned lying as a way of life.

But God performed a miracle in her heart at the age of twenty. He gave her a conscience. He gave her an altogether new and caring mind. She developed compassion and honesty. She learned how to cry. It did not and could not happen until Cathy turned her life completely into the hands of Jesus. Once she did that, by asking Him to be her Lord and Savior, a transformation that defies medicine and psychology took place. The same human being who had been selfish, heartless, dishonest and defiant became pure, open, honest and genuinely humble.

Cathy's life demonstrates the mercy of a loving God. She came to know her mother only briefly as an adult, but she had enough time to introduce her to the Lord Jesus before she died. She never had the mother she longed for, never experienced the loving home she dreamed of as a little girl. And so the Lord gave her *inside* what she missed on the outside: love, joy, peace, patience, kindness, goodness, gentleness, meekness and self-control.

We limit God when we forget the Bible's promise: "Though your father and mother forsake you, the Lord will take you up." If you were forsaken ten, twenty, even thirty years ago, the Lord will take you up now and heal every open wound, fill every crevice of your heart with himself and you will no longer be a victim of the tyranny of the past.

I know another woman who also didn't grow up in what we would call a loving traditional home. Her name is Charlie (a nickname her husband, Bob, gave her twenty years ago and it stuck). Charlie is a mother whose own daughter had to play mommy to *her*.

Charlie, today, is a wife, mother and grandmother. She is an effervescent, bubbly woman who gives you the impression she is always celebrating something you ought to know about. Her smile is luminous and it engulfs you, so when you are with Charlie and she is looking at you and laughing and energetically telling you about the Lord, you are a captive of a glowing rush of power, like standing next to a 100,000-volt power line.

Charlie didn't feel loved by her own mother as a little girl and, like Cathy, learned that discipline was a nasty word—a word that always meant pain and meaningless self-denial to meet someone else's demands.

Charlie and Bob are leaders of a Christian ministry to alcoholics. They are warm, compassionate and understanding people, like the perfect mom and dad. They weren't always. Charlie was not a perfect mother. She says, "I was so afraid of failing that I did."

I met Charlie in 1981 at a small, friendly church in Escondido, California, called Praise Center. There was a Mother-Daughter Banquet at the church, and as a special feature they had a Daughter of the Year contest. Charlie wrote a letter nominating her daughter, Errin, for the award. She showed me the letter and it so deeply impressed me that six years later I called her and asked if I could tell her story in this book.

With her consent, here it is.

"My daughter loved me, cared for me and defended me. . . ."

—*Charlie*

DAUGHTER OF THE YEAR

CHAPTER EIGHTEEN

"I nominate my daughter, Errin, as Daughter of the Year because she is every year.

The first eight years of her life I drank continuously and left home often.

So she was in charge of the house and brother who was four years younger than her.

My daughter loved me, cared for me and defended me.

The next ten years I stayed sober and also stayed home. Errin had polio, which had left her spine deformed. The doctor said she would never be a normal woman in physical growth or be able to bear children. She spent the next four years in and out of Children's Hospital, had to have fourteen inches of her spine fused solid so that it is impossible for her to bend her back. She was in a body cast for two and a half years which cut out all activity with the other children her age, but she never complained or made life difficult for me. She was always happy and cheerful and supportive of me. During part of this time I was pregnant with her youngest brother and when he was born she took over his care as if he had been sent to her.

When Errin was sixteen in high school and everything was going normal for her, she was in a bus accident and broke her back and we were told she would have to have another surgery and be in the cast again for two or three years.

But my daughter knew something I didn't know. She knew Jesus and claimed He would heal her. I thought she was dreaming and would be completely disillusioned, but she was right.

Jesus did heal her and she did not have to spend two years in a body cast.

But in 1970, her life completely changed because I started drinking again. Once more she became the mother. She worked full time at J. C. Penney, took care of a fifteen room house, helped her brothers with their homework, made sure they had birthday celebrations, normal and happy Christmases, and told them about the Lord Jesus who loved them.

Never once did her faith waver. She prayed for her mother, and believed one day I would be healed and delivered from alcoholism and we would all be a family again. She formed a group called Ala-Teens for young people with alcoholic parents. She told them and convinced them there was hope.

In June of 1973 Errin's prayers were answered. My daughter and I now share and love the same Jesus that she tried to tell me about all those years.

Errin had to teach me how to balance a budget, clean my house and all those things I should have taught her. But she raised her mother. And Jesus raised her. It was the Lord who taught and guided her because she had no one else.

Errin is married with a daughter of her own now and she is the kind of mother I always wanted to be to her but didn't know how.

My daughter, Errin, is not just my daughter, but my best friend.

Never once has she condemned me for the kind of life she lived or the things she missed out on.

. . . She loved me, cared for me . . . defended me.

Charlie"

There are those people
who drink
to drown their sorrow.
Somebody ought
to tell them
sorrow knows how to swim.[1]

---

[1]Adapted from an Ann Landers statement, *Field Newspaper Syndicate*, 1983.

THE CHILD AS MOTHER

CHAPTER NINETEEN

Charlie did her drinking at home. Alone. In the daytime. She drank anything alcoholic. Wine, beer, scotch—it didn't matter as long as it made her drunk. She hid the empty bottles in the clothes dryer or the toy box, places she knew her husband wouldn't look. The night before the trash collector came, she had to run around to all the neighbors' houses, depositing the empty bottles in their trash cans.

From the time Errin was about two and a half years old, she was already taking over the job of being mommy.

One day when Charlie was passed out on the sofa, she awoke to Errin's noises in the kitchen. She had a big bowl and had dumped everything from the refrigerator in it. Apples, oranges, catsup, jelly, milk, bread . . . She was proud of herself, grinning. "See, Mom? I'm making a cake!"

Another time when Charlie was passed out, Errin had bowls all over the floor, feeding the dog the leftover roast beef dinner from the night before. "Don't worry, Mom. I'm taking care of Fanny for you."

Charlie didn't think her daughter's attempts at being Mommy's helper were cute. When Errin painted her new ruffled dress with fingernail polish, Charlie awoke to a de-

lighted, "Hi, Mommy! Look what I made all by myself!"
Charlie was furious. She yelled. Spanked.

". . . My daughter loved me, cared for me and defended me. . . ."

Charlie's own mother had been a prostitute, a high-class one, she says, with wealthy clients. She was glamorous. Charlie only remembers being frightened, molested, abused, sent to stay with any relative who would have her. Her mother would send her away or take off for years at a time. Once her mother was gone for so long that when she came back, Charlie didn't know who she was. Someone said, "Well, aren't you going to say hello to your mother?" Charlie thought they were playing a joke on her.

She had a fantasy when she was a child. She dreamed of belonging to someone—a family who loved her, with a real house and furniture of their own, her own bed, toys.

Charlie told me, "I just can't put into words how alone I felt all the time. It was like I was encased in a big cake of ice. My mother beat me sometimes so bad I couldn't go to school the next day. All I can remember is fear.

"And being shut off from everything. Ice. It was like I lived in a big cake of ice and I was frozen in the middle of it. That's how it was."

Never anyone's legal foster child or legally adopted by any one family, Charlie moved from one relative to another. Relatives who never hugged. Never said encouraging things. Never ever said I love you.

When her father remarried she hoped maybe her dream for a home would come true.

It didn't.

But her father gave her something else. At a party at his house when he was quite drunk he said, "You want a drink, kid?" And Charlie, eager to please him, said yes. He poured her a straight shot of whiskey and she took that shot straight down just like she'd seen him do. He cheered and complimented her. She had earned his approval.

Something happened to Charlie at that moment that she would never forget. Her eyes watered, her throat and stomach burned, and suddenly the ice around her started to melt. She felt warm inside, as if a soft cocoon were slowly covering her. She could feel and taste the whiskey in her nose and the back of her head and she was at last *warm*. She was seven years old.

By the time Charlie was seventeen years old, she decided to make a career out of drinking. She would forever pursue the warmth of the cocoon and live to escape the iceberg.

She met Bob in a bar, and they were married in three weeks. Bob was a heavy drinker, too. But by now drinking was her best friend, the only friend in life she said she could depend on. Bob was from a deeply religious family. Charlie and Bob didn't fit in.

Charlie didn't trust people, because she believed everyone was better than she. So many ugly memories inside. Because of the ugly memories, *she* believed she was ugly. But people said she was beautiful. She even agreed to enter beauty contests, but she jeopardized her chances of winning or placing by getting drunk. That way she could prove she wasn't beautiful.

And she wasn't lovable either.

Her daughter, Errin, was born in 1951 and her son, Bobby, was born in 1955. She used the baby buggy to carry liquor home from the liquor stores. She stashed a six-pack from one liquor store in the diaper bag, the wine from another store under the baby, the hard liquor from yet another store in the blankets. Running from pain. Running from the ice. Looking for her cocoon. So many bottles in the buggy, there was hardly room for the baby.

Soon Charlie started to run away from home. Just leave a note on the table and walk out. The kids would be taking a nap, or at the store with their dad, or at their grandmother's, and Charlie would walk out the door and not look back. They'd never miss her, she thought. Bob's mother would take care of them.

She walked out on her babies, just like her mother had walked out on her. Only Charlie didn't head uptown to the exclusive hotels. She went directly to skid row. The one place where you didn't have to worry about earning approval.

Once she ran away for eight months.

Another time she ran away and joined a carnival.

Anyone who says fear cannot be stronger than goodness does not know much about fear. There is such power in fear that God tells us the *only* antidote for the poison of it is His love. Perfect love.

Fear is an evil thing. It demands perfection of us and the world around us. And when we come short of perfection, fear derides and torments us. Fear lies to us, tells us we're stupid, unattractive, weak, ineffectual, less important than others. Fear tells us that when others find out how bad we are, they'll hate us, maybe even hurt us.

Fear is impossible to live with. You have to numb it, deny it, repress it if you don't dare face it. It's a monster, a beast. Fear causes wars, deaths; it destroys homes, families, businesses, kingdoms, nations. Fear gives birth to despots and dictators and then feeds them with millions of spineless supporters. Fear builds bombs to blow up continents. It buys handguns for little old ladies to hide in their glove compartments. Fear is one of God's greatest enemies because it is a sin against innocence and faith.

Charlie joined Alcoholics Anonymous with Bob in 1959. For ten and a half years she stayed sober. Another baby came, a boy named Kelly. He was her Sober Baby, she says. Life was good. But the fears were still there. She didn't have her cocoon.

At the end of ten and a half years, she and Bob convinced themselves they didn't have drinking problems and they could be free to have an occasional drink.

Charlie was sitting on a plane with Errin beside her on the way to Florida where Bob was starting a new job. Charlie ordered a drink from the flight attendant and Errin went nuts. Became hysterical.

"Mom! I don't want you to die! Please! Don't drink!"

For the next three years while her mother stayed drunk, Errin did all of the housework, the cooking, the shopping. She made sure Kelly, who was only seven, got off to school, took care of Bobby, helped them both with their homework, and also held down a full-time job at J. C. Penny.

Charlie began running away again. She would file for divorce but never go through with it. She was out every night drinking. She lost her car several times a week, and never knew how she got home.

Each time Charlie came back home, she'd find Errin in complete charge of the house, the family's needs, just as if she was the faithful mother and Charlie was the prodigal child.

But Errin didn't show resentment to her mother. She hated her drinking and refused to excuse it, but she acted with respect and love for her mother. It was tough love and it was hard to take.

One night, Errin tracked her mother to the bar she had been drinking in all day. "Come on, Mom; you've got to get out of here. You've got to come home now." Charlie fought, protested, but Errin's strong will won over hers.

She allowed Errin to take her out to the car and put her in it. But when she stopped for a stop light at the corner, Charlie flung open the door and jumped out. Running back to the bar, she could hear Errin crying out to her, "Mom! Please! Please don't go back in there! Please, Mom!"

"And Errin never hated me. She never hated me."

Then a shocking thing happened in Charlie's life. Liquor stopped being her friend. It didn't take the bad memories away anymore. The ice, like knives, was back—thicker, deeper and colder. Drinking was no longer warm and co-coon-like. There was no friend in the glass. It was ugly and cruel.

Then came the voices. The screaming, macabre voices. Charlie heard them in the night, in the day. Migraines. Invisible voices laughing at her, giggling, leering.

They put her in the hospital. There were the shock treatments, the loss of time, confusion. Screaming voices in her head. Nobody there. There were words like "hopeless," "incurable," "vegetable." Bob and the kids came to visit Charlie in the hospital and she didn't know who they were.

Bob can't talk about Jesus today without crying. When he talks about what God did for Charlie and him, he cries so hard nobody can understand what he's saying. Jesus is more real to Charlie and Bob today than anything they can name on earth. The hate-busting power of Jesus not only saved Charlie from destroying herself and dying in the pit of hell, He restored her health and mind!

Religion had always seemed so hard, so legalistic to Bob and Charlie. They had never really thought of Him as a fair or decent sort of God. She had suffered too much. So had Bob. When he was a little boy, one of his first memories is trying to get his mother to hold him. He tried crawling on her lap, reaching for her, and she just wouldn't hold him. She *couldn't*.

Mothers don't know the important place they hold over the lives of their children. It wasn't until a lifetime of alcoholism and suffering that Bob finally learned through counseling that when his mother rejected him, something inside him said, "I'll never be rejected again." And so he always did the rejecting before anyone else did. Drinking assisted his rampage on an unyielding, unloving world.

But on a beautiful day in June 1973, Charlie and Bob asked the Lord Jesus to be Lord of their lives. God knew what it would take to bring them home to His loving arms. They felt His presence, *felt* and knew God was real. Slowly the voices left Charlie and never returned. Gradually her mind was restored. She could remember things again. Her body was without pain. She could sleep at night.

"The first time we tried to get sober we did it without the Lord Jesus. We had AA, and I see now that we needed Jesus first and AA second. Since the day I asked Jesus to be my Lord and Savior, I have not desired a drink. It's the truth. AA is wonderful and vitally important to us now that we know who our Higher Power is. Today Jesus is first in our lives.

"The day—in fact, the moment—I prayed and gave my heart and soul to the Lord Jesus, something incredible happened. A warmth came over me, a gentle embrace from the inside-out. Alcohol had numbed me, but this warmth was giving me life and energy. The ice cracked, chipped, broke into pieces from around my body and mind. I was no longer cold, no longer on the outside. I felt as though I was being held in His arms, and it's there I want to stay forever. At last I found my warm cocoon.

"I had to learn from my grown daughter how to do things like balancing a checkbook, grocery shop, clean the house. Drinking had robbed me of everything that gives a purpose and dignity.

"Now my daughter and I are best friends. She calls me for advice! She actually honors my opinion. I've even heard her say to her children, 'Go ask Grandma.'

"In the car on our way home from the Mother-Daughter Banquet the night Errin won Daughter of the Year, she said to me, 'Oh, Mom, I didn't have it so bad—really. I had *Jesus*.' "

I will always cry when I think of that moment and when I remember the horrible childhood I gave her. But God has forgiven me, and I must always remind myself of that.

"You want to hear something else beautiful? You want to hear how precious Jesus is? My little granddaughter will call me up now and say, 'Grandma, my girlfriend's mother is an alcoholic. Will you talk to her?' I tell her, 'Yes, if she wants someone to talk to, you tell her to call me. But in the meantime, you tell her I will be praying for her.'

"Two weeks ago my granddaughter telephoned, all excited, and said her friend's mother had finally admitted she had a problem and had gone to rehabilitation for treatment. My granddaughter said, 'She was happy because I told her *you* were praying for her, Grandma.'

"Errin loved me, cared for me . . . defended me . . ."

Now I want to live my life to love, care for and help others find what we have in the Lord Jesus. And maybe I can even be a true friend to Errin.

In evil long I took delight,
Unawed by shame and fear,
Till a new object struck my sight,
And stopped my wild career.
Amazing grace! how sweet the sound
That saved a wretch like me!
I once was lost, but now I'm found,
Was blind, but now I see.

—*John Newton*

FREE TO FORGIVE

CHAPTER TWENTY

When we want to know who God is, we look to His Word. When we ask, "Can God *ever* forgive me for what I've done?" whatever the sin may be, the answer is to be found in His Word, in which His character is revealed. In it we read how He declares himself merciful and loving.

In the Book of Exodus, Moses asks God, "Show me Thy glory." God didn't bash him over the head with a burning bush and tell him, "You've got a lot of nerve!" He answered, "I will make all My goodness pass before thee" (Ex. 33:18, 19). That's the infinite love of God. He wanted Moses to know Him for who He is: "The Lord, the Lord God, compassionate and gracious, slow to anger, and abounding in lovingkindness and truth" (Ex. 34:6).

Slow to anger. "Who keeps lovingkindness for thousands, who forgives iniquity, transgression and sin; yet He will by no means leave the guilty. . ." (Ex. 34:7).

The great relief and inexpressible joy at being cleansed and completely forgiven was an astounding experience for Charlie and Bob. Even today Charlie weeps, remembering her children coming home to an empty house when she had run away and left them. She can still hear them crying,

"Mama! Isn't anybody home? Mama?" But she can also hear, "As far as the east is from the west, so far has He removed our transgressions from us" (Ps. 103:12).

The exquisite relief and gratitude sears to a depth of our soul that we cannot reach ourselves. Forgiveness and mercy transform us, re-shape us. These are words at which we gasp in astonishment:

> Let the wicked forsake his way, and the unrighteous man his thoughts; and let him return to the Lord, and He will have love, pity, and mercy for him; and to our God, for He will multiply to him His abundant pardon. (Isa. 55:7, The Amplified Bible)

We sometimes confuse forgiveness with approval. God doesn't. He says, "Though your sins be as scarlet, they shall be white as snow" (Isa. 1:18). He despises the sin, but He loves the sinner.

"Errin wasn't an 'enabler,' a person who defends the alcoholic, helps him or her, makes excuses for him or her, and actually enables the alcoholic to stay one. Errin would tell people I had a drinking problem. She wouldn't lie for me. In helping other young people with alcoholic parents, she tells them to stop being enablers."

At times, however, we want our own way so desperately that we slap love in the face and accuse God of not caring.

> My little children, I write you these things so that you may not violate God's law and sin; but if any one should sin, we have an Advocate (One Who will intercede for us) with the Father; [it is] Jesus Christ [the all] righteous— upright, just, Who conforms to the Father's will in every purpose, thought and action. (1 John 2:1, The Amplified Bible)

God's sacrifice of unparalleled love was to give His only Son, Jesus Christ, to die a brutal death on a cross like a common thief *in our place*. We are the thieves, the murderers, the hateful, the jealous, the proud, the selfish. The Lord Jesus—perfect, pure and sinless—*became* sin in our place.

We are so dearly loved and prized by the Father that He made a way for us to be united in life with Him and His Spirit. Someone put it this way: "Christ was the medium through which He [God] could pour out His infinite love upon a fallen world."

So for a world that didn't love Him, He poured out His mercy, tenderness and forgiveness. People like Elaine turned from Him, didn't take His mercy. Charlie and Bob, their children, Bobby and Kelly, and Errin did. The Lord restores homes just as He restores hearts.

Yet I must make an important distinction here. We can feel genuinely sorry for our sin and still fail to understand the true nature of repentance. Many times a person can feel bad for wrongs they have committed. Many times we are quick to repair the wounds of our sins, or cover over the vastness of the sins to avoid personal pain. This is not repentance.

Esau was sorry and felt terrible when he realized he had sold his birthright for a bowl of stew. He feared how his wrongdoing was going to affect his future.

Balaam was quick to acknowledge his guilt in order to save his life when he met with an angel who stood in his path with a drawn sword.

And then there's Judas who felt bad after sending the King of Glory to His death. The Amplified Version of Matthew 27:3 says Judas Iscariot was afflicted in mind and troubled for his former folly; and with remorse (that is, an aftercare and little more than a selfish dread of the consequences). Terrified he cried out, "I have sinned in that I have betrayed innocent blood" (Matt. 27:4, The Amplified Bible).

Repentance is turning from sin. As mothers and daughters, we must face this choice daily. We must choose to keep a clean slate with the Lord.

His law is sacred.

His light illuminates our thoughts and intentions so that

we can reject and turn from those which are sinful. David taught us the true meaning of repentance:

> Have mercy upon me, O God, according to Your steadfast love; according to the multitude of Your tender mercies and lovingkindness blot out my transgressions. Wash me thoroughly [and repeatedly] from my iniquity and guilt, and cleanse me and make me wholly pure from my sin! For I am conscious of my transgressions and I acknowledge them; my sin is ever before me. Against You, You only, have I sinned, and done that which is evil in Your sight. (Ps. 51:1–4a, The Amplified Bible)

One of our best gifts from God is the ability He gives us to repent, to feel a broken and a contrite heart, to go the opposite way of sin and do the holy and right thing, based upon remorse and hatred of sin.

Repentance always means change. It means a change of mind and attitude. Forgiveness means freedom. It means letting go of hate and feeling good again.

If you're on the other end of forgiveness, you may be burning with anger, bitterness, resentment. You may be the wronged one. Perhaps your mother hurt you deeply. You sting. You cringe. You hurt.

Forgiveness doesn't always come easy. It's painful. Maybe you think your mother doesn't deserve your forgiveness. It's possible that you're confusing forgiveness with approval. Forgiveness doesn't require emotion. When someone hurts you, don't wait for feelings of compassion and tenderness before you forgive. You don't have to approve of your mother to forgive her. And you don't have to love your mother to forgive her. Just forgive.

Ask yourself the question, "Is unforgiveness good for me?"

Accept only that which is good for you according to God's Word. God brings into your life that which is good for you, that which is enriching, uplifting, comforting, strengthening (even trials and hardships). By choosing to accept what is good for you, you help and give good to others.

Unforgiveness will rob you.

Perhaps you need to forgive your daughter. Let her go. Release her to the Lord. She has hurt and disappointed you. Let her go.

Pray daily:

Lord Jesus, my daughter has hurt me. I forgive.

Lord, she has insulted me, refused my friendship. I forgive.

Lord, my daughter has behaved thoughtlessly and unkindly. I forgive.

Lord, my daughter hurts herself and behaves stupidly. She chooses poor relationships. In my opinion she is wasting her life. I forgive.

Forgiving does not mean condoning, nor does it mean approval.

The Apostle Paul called himself the chief of sinners. He wrote to the Christians in Colossae:

Be gentle and forbearing with one another and, if one has a difference (a grievance or complaint) against another, readily pardoning each other; even as the Lord has freely forgiven you, so must you also [forgive]. (Col. 3:13, The Amplified Bible)

Paul used a word for forgiven that was a form of the word grace. The Greek word for grace is *charis*, the root of *charizomai*, forgiveness. His forgiveness is sweet, full of love and unmerited favor. His forgiveness purifies us, makes us whole, and fills us with His joy.

The Lord is calling women to serve Him purely,

. wholly,

joyously.

We are of use to Him only if we have clean hands and a pure heart. We are never limited by our femininity, only by sin.

Queen Elizabeth I said, "I know I have the body of a

206 ■ MOTHERS & Daughters

weak and feeble woman, but I have the heart and stomach of a king."

If I were with you right now, we could take hands and pray together and repent of the heavy weights of
> unforgiveness
> shame
> guilt
> despair
> self-recrimination
> depression
> fear of failure
> remorse
> irresponsibility
> childishness
> bitterness
> jealousy

and every other devilish hindrance to our calling as mighty women of valor in the service of the Lord.

As mothers and daughters, let's engage in a holy fast in which we turn from the above enslavements and make the choices God has already chosen for us.

> Is not this the fast that I have chosen: to loose the bonds of wickedness, to undo the bands of the yoke, to let the oppressed go free, and that you break every [enslaving] yoke?" (Isa. 58:6, The Amplified Bible)

I choose this fast because I want to live a sanctified, holy life.

> I want to hear God, see God.
> I want to love the whole of God.
> I want to know the heart of God.
> I live to express the heart of God.
> I repent of all else.

Grandma, when you were young,
were you ever a mother?

—*Five-year-old Girl to Her Sixty-year-old,*
College Professor Grandmother

ON THE EDGE OF THE UNKNOWN

CHAPTER TWENTY-ONE

In our society we consider grandmothers ex-mothers. These are women who have finished a job. We permit them to have a hand in mothering and, spasmodically (in a modified way), reenact their own mothering experience with their grandchildren. In effect, Grandma is allowed to only play at mothering on the occasions the *real* mother needs help or cannot cope.

"We have not discovered what to do with our ex-mothers," writes Sheila Kitzinger.[1] ". . . for those women who have never had the opportunities of education which will fit them for later careers, who are not easily employable outside the home, or who lack the initiative and confidence to seek outside interests, the thirty years they can expect after mothering is over may be very empty and purposeless."

In women, depression is more common after the age of forty than before. The grieving over loss of youth, loss of purpose and without a family who needs her is overwhelming. It is this age group of women who fall prey to domestic alcoholism, the wine and whiskey bottles under the sink,

---

[1]Sheila Kitzinger, *Women As Mothers* (New York: Random House, 1978).

and the TV set going most of the day and night. These are the women who no longer feel needed by anybody and retreat into avoidance behavior rather than doing something about their lives.

But we control our own destiny—that is to say, *we* are the navigators of our own ships. Even if we're unable to walk, or if we're the daughter of a portentous alcoholic, we can still touch our world and create something beautiful of the time we're allotted here.

I am personally committed to living on what I call the edge of the unknown.

C. S. Lewis, in his book *The Four Loves*, talks about "need-love" and "gift-love." Our love for God is need-love, and when directed toward Him, it is right and holy. "Gift-love" is another love, the kind that must give. I think of Lewis's words as perfectly aimed at the grandmother:

> . . . the proper aim of giving is to put the recipient in a state where he no longer needs our gift. We feed children in order that they may soon be able to feed themselves; we teach them in order that they may soon not need our teaching. Thus a heavy task is laid upon this Gift-love. It must work towards its own abdication. We must aim at making ourselves superfluous. The hour when we can say "They need me no longer" should be our reward.[2]

The Apostle Paul said:

> One thing I do—it is my one aspiration: forgetting what lies behind and straining forward to what lies ahead, I press toward the goal to win the [supreme and heavenly] prize to which God in Christ is calling us upward. (Phil. 3:13–14, The Amplified Bible)

If we see ourselves as women of God pressing toward the holy prize when we are young, we will continue to see ourselves pressing on when we are older. Being young is our preparation for being old!

---

[2]C.S. Lewis, *The Four Loves* (New York: Harcourt Brace & World, 1960).

The Christian woman lives by the words of the Apostle Paul at every age of her life:

> I have strength for all things in Christ Who empowers me—I am ready for anything and equal to anything through Him Who infuses inner strength into me, [that is, I am self-sufficient in Christ's sufficiency]. (Phil. 4:13, The Amplified Bible)

In Japan, old age is treated differently than in the West. At the age of sixty-one a party is given, and from this time on a grandmother must be treated with great consideration; everything she asks for must be given her, her opinions are listened to with respect, and she should never be criticized. Grandma can now wear red, the color of childhood. Old age to the Japanese is not a disability to ignore, but a triumph, and a vantage point attained at last at the end of the long road of child-rearing.

For you and me, our dignity is not attained through age but through our own developed wisdom and experience. I have never met a foolish, naive and helpless woman who has walked intimately with the Lord for many years. Knowing Jesus is to absorb strength and wisdom. He gives us integrity, self-esteem, *ability*. He gives us the components of self-esteem: a sense of belonging, a sense of worth and a sense of capability.

> Have you not known? Have you not heard? The everlasting God, the Lord, the Creator of the ends of the earth, does not faint or grow weary. . . . He gives power to the faint and weary, and to him [and her] who has no might He increases strength—causing it to multiply and making it abound. (Isa. 40:28a-29)

We should look forward to our forties, fifties, sixties, seventies and eighties with high hopes. Think how assertive we'll be. Think how much we will have read, how many conflicts we will have solved, how many battles we will have won. Think how terrific we'll look in red!

Growing old is the unknown.

Lord, help me to live comfortably on the edge of the unknown.

The following is a dialogue I had with my own mother, and it gave me much insight into her own heart as well as the process of aging.

Me: Mom, which do you think of yourself as—a mother or a daughter?

Mother: When I'm with you, I'm a mother.

Me: But how about when you're alone?

Mother: When I'm alone, I'm Dorothy.

Me: And when you're with your grandchildren, you're a grandmother?

Mother: Yes, but I don't actually think, "Now I'm being a grandmother."

Me: Do you have a favorite role?

Mother: I like being Dorothy, but my favorite roles are wife and mother. Together. I'm from the generation where women didn't feel like women if they weren't wife and mother. My least favorite role is being a widow. That would be right now. I was happiest when your father was alive and it was the two of us together with our children. We had hopes and dreams ahead of us. Hope for you, for us. Even on the very day of the accident when your father was killed, we had hopes and dreams ahead of us. It was wonderful being a wife and mother. Yes, my very favorite time of life was when your father was alive and you children were home. We were all a part of one another's lives. Your daily plans and activities were all a part of our daily plans and activities. We were together and that was the best time of my life.

Me: How about now?

Mother: Now I am a widow.

Me: But how about "mother"? You're still a mother.

Mother: Now, as a mother, I feel close to my children. But I am not a part of your lives, your daily plans and activities. The time when your life was a part of mine is gone. It's the way it should be, of course, but it means a lot of adjusting. The role "mother" is not always before me and on my mind. It doesn't dictate my actions during the day. My children are grown and on their own. I feel close to you and your brother and sister. I'm happy with your success, Marie. You serve the Lord with your whole heart. You're genuine and I enjoy watching you live and teach what you believe.

Me: What's the thing you're happiest about?

Mother: I like it that you grew up! You didn't remain a child into your adult years. You're capable, smart and serving God. You sort of defied the system for girls.

Me: Anything else?

Mother: I'm proudest of you when you're happy. I must say I'm perfectly satisfied with each of my children. We're more than best friends. I can't explain it. We're far more personal than friends. We're part of each other. Your sister and your brother and you are the closest people in the world to me. You know how it is with your own children, Marie. The three of you are just closer than close.

My mother lives in a senior citizens' high-rise building, and she tells me stories about life there, the other people and what it's like to live without youth around. I learn more about getting old from her than from all the gerontology and psychology of aging studies I did in graduate school. She told me the following story:

"In my building I see mothers downstairs in the lobby waiting for their daughters to come to take them to their homes, or to some doings, or shopping. And most of the time, the daughters have protective authoritative-patient (or *impatient*, depending on the character of the daughter) attitudes. And there's the mother, a more resigned or cantankerous (depending on the character of the mother) woman ready to follow along after the daughter, sometimes eager to please, like a puppy.

"And I watch the daughter who is often still like a child, trying to prove to her mother that she is grown-up and capable and worthy of respect. The old woman doesn't recognize how desperately her daughter is working for her approval. So when she insists she carry her own shopping bag, the daughter argues.

" 'Let *me* carry that.'

" 'No, I can carry it myself. I'm not helpless.'

" 'I didn't say you were helpless. I'm only trying to save you the trouble.'

" 'I can carry my own bag!'

" 'All right. All right. Have it your way. Just don't complain to me and call me up to take you to the doctor when you pull your back out.'

"So for her attempts at self-sufficiency, the mother is punished and feels rejected. The daughter, in turn, feels unappreciated. It's a sorry situation.

"Just the other day I was coming in through the front door in the lobby and I met an old woman shuffling toward the elevator. She looked a little forlorn. She turned to me and explained that the elevator was on the sixth floor because her daughter had gone ahead of her and taken it up without her. As we waited together for the elevator's return, she said her daughter didn't wait for her because she took too long. She sighed such a pathetic, resigned sigh and said, 'They're always in a hurry.' I felt terrible for her."

That story made me sad. I meditated on it for a couple of days, and decided daughters would not do that to mothers in later years if they didn't get away with being selfish and thoughtless toward her in earlier years. One forty-year-old daughter told me, "At last I can treat my mother as inflexibly as she always treated me!"

I can see myself as an old lady sprinting up the six flights of stairs, beating the elevator (I've actually done this many, many times but always in fun) and shouting at the thoughtless dolts who left me behind, "Do that again to me and I'm taking the Porsche and moving to Miami."

Communication. Talking. Telling each other how you feel, how you think. It's vitally important to describe your feelings as a grandmother, as a woman who has reached the golden years we're all heading toward.

My mother told me, "You feel bad about the woman and the shopping bag because you can see how little true communication there is between the mother and daughter. But as for the woman at the elevator, I want you to see that even though you believe you would never leave me, never abandon me, you already have."

My mouth fell. When did I *ever* leave my mother? I racked my brain trying to recall the thousands of distant elevators of the past.

"Let me explain," Mom said. "You leave me daily to run your own life, which, although you include me in it, I have no important say-so in things. I make no decisions, no important plans. You're good to me, heaven knows, but your life is yours and if you were to leave me at the elevator, I would have no recourse but to push the button and dolefully follow you. Oh, I could protest, but still, it wouldn't change the fact that you are the decision-maker. My children now make the decisions. The roles have reversed."

She was right. When I take her on trips or do the things for her I think are so special, it's my doing, my decision, on my time, at my convenience. Because of our economic situation, her children are now the ones who determine where to eat, what vacations to take, how much to spend and what gifts she gets.

I told her, in shame, really, "I'm going to include you

in decision-making and planning from now on wherever I can, and especially when it involves you. Let's walk up the six flights instead of taking the elevator, OK?"

She said, laughing, "There are certain things that cannot be changed, Marie. And I love you for working so hard to keep me young."

Then my mother—who adores my wonderful brother, Bill, and my precious sister, Corrine—said to me the sweetest words, "What a darling gift from God you are to me, my daughter, Marie."

Getting-Older Tips From a Grandmother:

1. "Gift-love" your family.
2. Tell your family you want to be included in family decisions when it pertains to you. Decisions including what restaurant to eat at on a night they're taking you out for dinner, or what time you want them to drop over when they say they'd like to see you. Give them a list of things you'd like for Christmas and your birthday. Tell them when you want to carry your own shopping bag and never let them leave you at the elevator.
3. Make one-year, five-year and ten-year goals (and beyond!) for yourself. Make it a detailed plan. Include vocational, recreational, educational, social and family goals. Each category has its own systematic plan. For example, if a five-year educational goal is to get a degree in art, you would list under your one-year educational goal plan: *Register for classes at the college and see a counselor about my schedule.* Under your five-year plan you may have as a vocational goal: *My first one-woman exhibit of paintings.* In between are the steps you take to get there.
4. Enlarge your social sphere. Don't depend on your family to provide your primary socialization. It may be disappointing. Find people your age with similar interests and

enjoy! You find these people in adult education classes, groups and activities; in the innumerable events sponsored at the senior citizens centers, in the universities and colleges offering continuing education courses and programs; through neighborhood interests groups, and finally, most importantly, through the church. It is crucial to be involved in an active, vital church with opportunities to serve and learn and enjoy enriching fellowship. At your age, you should be the joy and treasure of the young in Christ.

5. Dedicate this time in your life to penetrating deeper into God's Word and fellowship with Him. Make it your time of life to visit the throne of God more eagerly and frequently than ever before and prove His words, "My peace I give unto you: not as the world giveth, give I unto you. Let not your heart be troubled, neither let it be afraid" (John 14:27).

6. Don't allow your health to be your major concern and point of conversation. See yourself as a happy, peaceful, healthy, and joyful woman of God, no matter what medication you're on or what limitations your body may be giving you.

7. Endeavor to not allow the past to seem more important to you than the present. We value the good experiences of the past, but we must also appreciate the present or we won't experience it.

8. Forbid complaining, fault-finding and deriding discussions about how the world is going to the dogs and how bad youth is today. Be a person of hope and joy. Tell yourself every day the words Jesus has given to you, "These things have I spoken unto you, that my joy might remain in you, and that your joy might be full" (John 15:11).

9. Live comfortably on the edge of the unknown.

*God is faithful—reliable,
trustworthy and [therefore] ever
true to His promise, and He can be
depended on; by Him you were
called into companionship and
participation with His Son, Jesus
Christ our Lord.*

—1 Corinthians 1:9, The Amplified Bible)

INDIVIDUALITY

CHAPTER TWENTY-TWO

While writing this book, I met two delightful women on an airplane on my way from Fort Meyers, Florida, to Dallas, Texas. They were returning from a week of shell-hunting on an island off the Florida coast and I was on my way home after a speaking engagement.

The women, both widows and in their seventies, wore backpacks, tennis shoes, heavy jackets and jogging suits. (Hardly your typical grandmotherly attire.)

They talked to me about being mothers, grandmothers and "older" women. "We don't say *old*," said Belle, a woman with assailing eyes and wearing a rumpled, maroon jogging suit. "We say old*er*."

Kate, bespectacled and wearing a pair of loose-fitting red jeans, told me how their lives have gone through a metamorphosis. "For instance, we went to rent canoes the other day. Now, I've canoed all my life. But the man who gave us the canoe felt obligated to warn us about the hazards of canoeing and capsizing until I actually began to be a little afraid! Once we got out in the water, we realized it was only about four feet deep. Think of it."

Belle, wrinkling her nose, added, "And you'd think we'd

219

never driven a car in our lives either. We got instructions and warnings from everyone, and we've had drivers' licenses for fifty years!

"Marie, getting older is a matter of diminishing power. I, for one, don't like it and I'm fighting back."

I asked Belle how she fights back and she told me with her bright eyes flashing, "I don't allow myself to be forced into a *child* role. I refuse to allow myself to lose my sense of individuality and my right to independence."

Kate interjected, "I don't go for this reversal of roles business just because a person gets old*er*. I refuse to be narrowed to one dimension—age."

I was curious how their daughters felt about their mothers' independence and refusal to be "taken care of."

Belle answered first. "My daughter did something quite wonderful one day a couple of years ago. She sat down and figured out all the ways we are and are not alike. She seemed better able to feel herself whole and complete and to accept me after that. She seemed to better enjoy our relationship, too. I guess she discovered we are alike in some ways and not in others, but most of all, we're *separate* human beings."

Kate told me her daughter can't accept her refusal to be mothered. "She wants to tell me how to live. Calls up and asks what I'm eating and if I'm wearing a warm-enough jacket when I go out for my walks. She even watches for my yearly medical checkups. I tell her she must allow me my independence, and if I want to miss my doctor's appointment, wear T-shirts and shorts in the winter and eat nothing but tortilla chips, that's my business."

As I listened, I thought of my daughters, Christa and Liza, of the women I've written about in this book, Elaine, Bobbie, Sharon, Charlie and Errin. . . . Is this what they have to look forward to? Being old*er* and fighting for independence and the right to make their own decisions? Will they, in their white-haired years, return to the state of childishness, helpless and whining, only to be taken care of by others who are younger and more mobile?

Personally, I'd like to be on the beach writing about shells.

The flight went quickly as I listened to these two energetic, intelligent women talk. Lovers of the beach, we talked about tides, sand, stones, rocks, shells. "Did you know that not a single shell is like another?" We discussed books, music, left-brain, right-brain techniques of learning. And they talked about their roles as women, as daughters and mothers.

"If I had it to do over again, I think I would enjoy mothering more. I would take more pauses. I would count more stars with my daughter."

"I'd collect shells with her," Belle added. "So much of the beauty of life I discovered when I was old*er*. It's too bad, but it's true."

I sighed and was glad I was yet young enough to count the stars with my daughters. And in engaging in such a preposterous task, we would find something funny in it. We would probably fall all over each other hysterically, screaming with laughter. I can hear Liza, "What are we doing this for?"

And so this brings me to the importance of having fun and laughing with our mothers and daughters. Children laugh up to 500 times a day. Adults laugh maybe five times a.day—if that. When I talk about laughing, I mean side-holding, knee-slapping, uncontrollable *laughing*. Laughter is not the same as chuckling, giggling, grinning or smiling.

Research shows that laughter is a form of catharsis. It purges emotion, increases the heart rate, circulation and respiration. It's *good* for us.

Laughing together as a family is important. Not laughing *at* each other, but *with* each other. I treasure the hilarity I share with my daughters. Liza makes me laugh so hard when we're together, the tears splash on the floor. Many is the night we laugh into the wee hours as we engage in utter madness.

We love to stage dramatizations of our favorite characters and situations and we become so hysterical at ourselves, we're rendered limp with laughter. Experts say just *seconds* of this kind of laughter is equal to the cardiovascular benefits of a three-minute aerobic workout.

We have always laughed together and always will. I think my daughters are funny. They think I'm funny. Together we laugh at one another's stories, we laugh at ourselves and we don't try to top each other or compete for laughs. We don't work at being cleverer or wittier; we enjoy a natural flow of humor. I know some people whose aim it is to be the funniest, the wittiest. I may laugh at their jokes, but being with them is not fun; it's tiring.

I've often advised couples, in correlation with their counseling, to laugh together. It's amazing how difficult many of them have doing this. Some don't succeed at all.

"What's to laugh about?" they'll ask me in bewildered tones.

In the tanned faces of Kate and Belle, the years of laughter, of enjoying life and of sharing their delight and curiosity were clearly evident. Happiness is a great gift to give our daughters and to receive from our mothers.

I like these words by Susan Polis Schultz:

Thanks, Mom

Since I had a mother
whose many interests
kept her excited and occupied

Since I had a mother
who interacted with so many people
that she had a real feeling for the world

Since I had a mother
who always was strong
through any period of suffering

Since I had a mother
who was a complete person,
I always had a model

to look up to
and that made it easier
for me to develop into
an independent woman.[1]

This tribute is the product of the blessings we give our daughters. It also represents the sensitivity of the daughter and her ability to receive that which is good from her mother. I'd like to add, "Since I had a mother who introduced me to Jesus, I was able to grow up strong and whole."

In closing, I want to strongly encourage you to pray these Scripture-prayers for your daughter:

Lord, You will command Your lovingkindness in the daytime toward my precious daughter. And in the night Your song shall be with her, and her prayer will be directed to You, the God of her life all of her life. (Ps. 41:8)

Lord, you have called my daughter by name. She is Yours! When my daughter passes through the waters, You will be with her; and when she passes through the rivers, they will not overflow her. When she walks through the fire, she will not be scorched, nor will the flame burn her. For You are the Lord, her God, the Holy One of Israel, her Savior. (Isa. 43:1b–3a).

Pray this Scripture-prayer for your mother:

You, Lord, are righteous in all Your ways, and kind in all Your deeds. You, Lord, are near to my mother when she calls upon You. You will fulfill the desire of my mother, who fears and reverences You. You will always hear her cry and save her. You, Lord, keep my mother who loves You. (Ps. 145:17–20a)

Pray these Scriptures for yourself:

Blessed be the Lord, my rock, who trains my hands for war, and my fingers for battle. Lord, you are my lovingkindness and my fortress. You are my stronghold and

---

[1] Susan Polis Schultz, *I Want to Laugh, I Want to Cry* (Blue Mountain Arts, Inc., © Continental Publications, 1973).

my deliverer. You are my shield and You are He in whom
I take refuge. I have found You and therefore found life.
I have obtained favor from You. I will bless your name
forever and ever. (Ps. 144:1–2; Prov. 8:35)

And, Lord, I will never again minimize my personal
strengths as trivial. I will never again take weakness as a way
out of responsibility. I will never again neglect to laugh as I
count the stars with my mother and my daughters. . . . And
we will never again forget to gather shells, each one individual, as different and lovely as we are.